POWER TRADING

OLIVER L. VELEZ

Marketplace Books
Columbia, Maryland

ISBN: 1-59280-333-4
ISBN 13: 978-1-59280-333-0
Printed in the United States of America.

Table of Contents
Power Trading

How to Read This Book

This guidebook brings together three trading approaches that have been used by tens of thousands of traders who have participated in educational sessions presented by Oliver Velez and the Pristine team. The whole, in this case, is truly much greater than the sum of the parts.

Watch the DVD

The DVD in the back of this book brings you right into those sessions that have helped many traders access this powerful information. By using the DVD, you can watch the instructions again and again to absorb every concept, without ever having to leave home.

Read the Guidebook

The material in the next 300+ pages puts all of the information together into a visual roadmap that shows you how to apply the tactics and strategies that are covered in this multimedia learning experience.

Take the Online Tests

To realize the full potential of the information you have before you, we strongly encourage you to watch the DVD, read the book, and then go online and take the self tests. This guidebook was designed to help you easily identify the plays that will work best with your trading style, your personality, and your current portfolio.

Highly respected as one of the most eloquent trading educators in the business, Oliver engages you and walks you through the plays in each of these approaches in simple, accessible language. The guidebook format ensures that you will have detailed and instant access to Oliver's full library of information. You will now be able to reach over and flip directly to the play that will apply to today's market and use the highly developed approach that will best accomplish your trading goals.

Preface

You have known one truth since your first trade, or perhaps even before you ever hit the buy button. And, you are reminded of this unquestionable truth every day you are in or near the markets. It is simply: Markets are constantly changing. The very moment you are lulled into complacency, you will be harshly reminded of the tidal force that one small change in the markets can bring to bear on your trading mentality, profitability, and goals.

Yet, in spite of this evolving target, success is always within reach. A down day should not break a trader. By accepting the certainty of change, winning traders will see a down day as the voice of the market speaking to them. It is saying that the path to success has moved and if that they want to find success, they must change with the market. The winning patterns that materialized on the charts just yesterday are still there, but like a chameleon, they have mastered the art of camouflage and are challenging you to find them.

The analogies for having a collection of trading strategies to reach for when the markets shift are endless. Craftsmen have a wide variety of tools; fishermen have a selection of different baits or lures in their tackle box; artists begin with pallets of various colors—all of them must be ready for any changes that will come between them and their goals. To be masters of their skills, they know that they can't just bring every tool, lure, or color with them every day. They have to understand the value of every resource they bring along.

And as is true in any arena, the rookies are easy to spot. They are the ones at the dock whose boats are about to sink from overloading, or the hikers with packs so heavy they can't walk. On the other hand, the master will have a modest, yet very carefully selected collection of tools. There will be a very distinct and logical reason for each resource he or she has chosen. It will be proven, or meet some need he has identified in a past experience. The master will have seen it work and will know when and just how to optimally use the tool.

In trading, it is a matter of collecting the tactics that are proven and that provide the flexibility to adapt to changing market conditions. Master traders spend years honing their collection of tactics. Their tools may be certain pattern set-ups or different technical indicators, but no matter what, master traders build them into their trading styles because they work consistently for them. To gain access to a master's tools and why he has chosen each one is an unparalleled opportunity.

For the new trader, it can save immense amounts of time and money. The risks of missing an opportunity by not having the right strategy or by using the wrong one are very real and, to a certain extent, unavoidable. To be able to minimize that risk and accelerate the learning curve means a shorter distance to the income and freedom that attracts most people to trading.

For the experienced trader, even another master, it can offer a chance to augment an already powerful arsenal. Any new tactic should be held to the highest level of critique. Advanced traders have a clear idea of what they expect and they also know exactly what they need a new tool to accomplish. Their broader awareness of the market will have taught them that they need to constantly be looking out for and evaluating new ways to remain successful. With very specific and critical expectations, finding new tactics that are even worth testing can be tedious.

That's where this book comes into play. The collection of tactics included in this guide is designed to work in a variety of market conditions and to offer solutions that fit multiple trading styles.

In uncertain markets, guerrilla trading shows you how to block out the noise and zero in on individual setups that can be hidden by nebulous, undefined trends. Because they are frequently driven by market emotion, they can result in big, very quick moves. The key is to use a technical approach to see past the emotion and to directly target the profit.

Micro trading is a style that uses intraday charts and involves exiting all trades by the end of the day. It employs most of the strategies found in other approaches, but plays them at a much faster pace. For the high energy trader, micro trading will keep you engaged and will fit well with your trading personality.

Core trades can be held for a few weeks to a few months. Often used on key stocks and indexes that mimic the market, these plays fit well with Exchange Traded Funds. The key to core trading is to open up the time frames and use selected technical indicators to place the most effective entries and exits.

Each section includes the tactics that have proven most effective for each particular approach. Take full advantage of the information here by reading the text, watching the DVD, and taking the tests. You'll find then that you will understand and recognize clear opportunities in the market and you will have the right tactics to exploit every move the market makes. When difficult markets prevail, this arsenal of choices will provide you with new ways to find those elusive winning trades.

Change is always present in the markets, yet change always presents opportunities. Whether it is the information in this book or some other experience, keep searching and carefully select new tactics to keep with you as you trade.

—John Boyer, Vice President and General Manager,
Marketplace Books and Traders Library

Meet Oliver Velez

Oliver L. Velez, best selling author, trader, advisor, and entrepreneur, is one of the most sought after speakers and teachers on the subject of trading financial markets for a living. His seminars and speaking events have been attended by more than 60,000 traders all over the world, and his runaway best selling books, *Strategies for Profiting on Every Trade* and *Tools and Tactics of the Master Day Trader*, are considered must-read classics for anyone interested in trading markets for a living. Dow Jones dubbed him "the messiah of day trading" and financial programs on *CNBC*, *Bloomberg* and *Fox News* frequently seek out his expertise. Mr. Velez and his life-long dedication to bringing more awareness to trading as a way of life, have been favorably mentioned in the *New York Times*, the *Wall Street Journal*, *Barron's*, *Forbes*, *Stocks & Commodities* and a whole host of other financial publications. He has also been the subject of numerous articles and books written about Wall Street's most successful traders, including the popular book, *Bulls, Bears and Brains.*

Oliver L. Velez is internationally known for founding and growing Pristine Capital Holdings, Inc. (a firm he started out of his New York City basement apartment) into one of the country's premier educational institutions for investors and self-directed, retail traders. After serving as Pristine's Chairman and CEO for 12 years, Mr. Velez decided to turn his full attention to the professional trading arena. His new training program called Trade for Life™, which includes a 2-day seminar and 5-day Live Trading Session with Mr. Velez himself, is designed to train traders to go beyond retail to trade the markets professionally.

Today, Mr. Velez runs Velez Capital Management, LLC ("VCM"), one of the country's fastest growing private equity trading firms. VCM currently employs 260 professional traders who have been meticulously trained to trade his own personal account. Mr. Velez financially backs each one of his traders, absorbing all their losses, while sharing in the gains with the trader. Mr. Velez' vision is to grow his professional team of traders to more than 1,000 globally over the next 3 years. For the past 19 years, he has espoused the revolutionary idea that "micro trading," like "micro banking" has the potential to serve as a solution to many of the world's social ills. Through VCM and the Velez Family Foundation, Mr. Velez will be opening up trading divisions and training centers in Beijing, Vietnam, Moscow and Mexico City. More major cities throughout the world will be added in the future.

POWER TRADING

Winning Guerrilla, Micro, and Core Tactics

OLIVER L. VELEZ

PART 1
Guerrilla Trading

Chapter 1

An Introduction to Guerrilla Trading

Guerrilla trading is the most practiced and most dynamic form of market play that Pristine-trained traders utilize to take advantage of the markets. The guerrilla trading style is also perhaps the most interesting of all the trading styles. To begin, I would like to outline the five reasons why guerrilla trading is unique.

1. Guerrilla Tools Are Easy to Understand

In the other styles of trading, we take a long time learning about the trend and the general flow of the stock. This is not true for guerrilla trading. The best guerrilla trades almost can be thought of as occurring in a vacuum.

2. Guerrilla Trading Works Best in Uncertain Markets

Incredibly, guerrilla trades actually work best in sloppy, choppy, or non-trending markets. Because most of the other styles of play revolve around a trend or around the formation of precise patterns, the guerrilla style of trading dovetails perfectly as a complement to these other forms. When the market proves difficult for other forms of trading, it is often the guerrilla patterns that can save the day.

3. Guerrilla Trades Follow Their Own Course

Third, these trades usually have very low correlation to the market. One of the classic questions with virtually all other styles of trading is how to handle a situation in which you have a strong stock in a weak market or a weak stock in a strong market. You need to incorporate a market view in your game plan and decide if a strong stock is a good long play, or if the market will eventually break down a stock that temporarily appears to be strong. When a guerrilla play sets up properly, it often trades on its own with very little influence from the broader market.

4. Guerrilla Trading Plays off Other's Emotions to Win

If you've heard me talk before, or if you have read any of my prior writings, you'll likely know I believe that when we play stocks, we play people. It is not the fundamentals, the earnings statements, or the comments by CEOs or analysts that give us an opportunity to make money. Your ability to be a successful stock trader will be related to how well you can understand the emotional states of the people behind the buy and sell buttons. Guerrilla trading is the perfect example of this. Many of these guerrilla plays move quickly in a short period without regard to the current trend of the day. Some of the guerrilla plays deliver what we call "shock value," which creates a situation in which we have an edge.

> Guerrilla trades play on fear and greed more than any other strategy.

5. Guerrilla Trades are Trend-Neutral

And finally, this style of trading is unique because it is trend-neutral. Other than guerrilla, there is only one other tactic we use to fight the trend. It is known as a Climactic Buy Setup or Climactic Sell Setup (which will be discussed further in our core trading section). The Climactic setups are used 8% of the time to buck the prevailing trend. The guerrilla setups are not designed to specifically play with the trend or against the trend. They are trend-neutral.

However, by the very nature of their setups, many of them do fight the trend. The ones that fight the trend get their power from the fact that they're fighting the trend. The current move becomes more powerful than the prior trend of the stock and actually reverses the stock on a long-term basis.

> Guerrilla trades are "trend-neutral," so they can be played even if the play goes against the current trend.

The Charts Do Not Lie

Guerrilla trading, like the other styles of trading in the Pristine Method, revolves around technical analysis. We look at chart patterns to find particular setups. The price pattern of the chart contains all of the relevant fundamental data. Charts are the only things that do not lie.

Because of these facts, we are not interested in fundamental data, or analyst comments, or promises by CEOs. Many of the chart patterns formed by the guerrilla style of trading exemplify this concept more than any other style. You will see stocks that gap up on good news or a great earnings report, and then sell off for weeks. You will see certain gaps that literally change the trend of the daily and weekly charts for weeks and months to come.

Targets and Stops

I want to point out a couple of things that are similar to most of the guerrilla plays. First, let's discuss the concept of targets.

Many of the other styles of play that I teach have very defined target areas. That is because the tactic occurs inside a pre-defined structure—there is a pattern we look for to play the stock.

This is not the case with the guerrilla setups. The only pattern we look for goes back two bars. This means, in some cases, the target area will depend on the prior chart, which will be different in every case. Most of the target criteria in the strategies are fairly general. You'll need to look at each individual chart or dive into a lower time frame to find more exact target areas. I'll show you examples of how to do this.

Many of the guerrilla tactics involve using a very wide stop. This wide stop is many times justified because the guerrilla tactics often cause very large moves. However, you need to have a full understanding of money management and share-sizing policies. Remember that not all plays are supposed to be winners. We play the odds. The reason you make money at the end of the day is because the plays that do not work stopped at an appropriate area and the appropriate amount of money.

Also, if you play a large share size with a wide stop and that play proves to be one of the losers, you'll suffer a very large dollar loss. You should never do that. Always look at the size of the stop and play a share size that makes sense for your account size and projected loss per trade.

A Look at Gaps

One of the great things about the Pristine Method is that the strategies apply to any time frame. We use charts to see the reactions of people in order to read the emotional state of the market. These emotional states can be seen on every individual time frame. Generally speaking, the tactics we teach can be used on a monthly chart or on a 2-minute chart or anything in between.

Several of these guerrilla tactics involve gaps, and when we talk about a gap, we are talking about something that happens on a daily chart. Occasionally these tactics can be applied to the hourly chart, but for the most part we're talking about gaps that occur on the daily chart.

A gap is a term used to describe the condition when a stock opens at a significantly higher or lower price than it closed the prior day. The word gap refers to the empty space that is left on the daily chart from yesterday's close to today's open. However, gaps can also gap into the prior day's trading range, making it less obvious on a daily chart. Gaps can be either up or down. They can happen to all stocks, whether they are on the listed exchange or on the NASDAQ stock exchange (NASDAQ).

The gap is measured from the prior day's 4:00 p.m. closing price to the current day's 9:30 a.m. opening price. All times I refer to are Eastern Standard Time (EST). The pre- and post-market activity does not affect the gap for our purposes. Stocks can trade pre-market starting at 8:00 a.m. and after market hours until 8:00

p.m. through Electronic Communication Networks, but these are not considered normal market hours. Many stocks may gap a small amount every day, but our focus is on those gapping significantly.

> Gaps are measured from the regular market close of the prior session until the regular market open of the current day.

For example, stock XYZ closes at 4:00 p.m. EST at 37. It trades in after market hours up to 38. The next day at 8:00 a.m. EST, it starts trading at 38.5 and trades up to 39.5. By 9:30, the stock is all the way back down to 37.10. The gap, as we measure it, is only 10 cents. All of the post-market and pre-market trades do not matter in determining whether a stock is gapping, though you may want to be aware of those trades when planning a strategy. The stock traded, and people made and lost money, but the gap was not affected.

Gaps are usually driven by the news. Individual stocks can gap up or down due to news such as earnings reports, earnings pre-announcements, analysts' upgrades and downgrades, rumors, message board posts, CNBC, or key people in the company commenting or buying/selling the company stock.

Groups of stocks or the whole market may gap up or down due to various economic reports, news on the economy, political news, or major world events (like the large gap down from 9/11). This news can cause many individual issues to gap with the market. Many big name stocks move very closely with the market. Some may be in the sectors that are most affected by the news.

Whatever the reason, the result is that either buying or selling pressure at open the next day will make the stock open at a different price than where it closed. Why are gaps important? This sudden change in demand is often the beginning of a major move.

Hit and Run Approach

Guerrilla trading is a very dynamic style, and one of the most active styles of market play. It calls for holding stocks anywhere from several hours to a day or two. The guerrilla style of market play can be referred to as the hit-and-run approach to the market. Buy a stock on Monday and sell it on Tuesday. Short a stock on Thursday and cover Friday. It is that hit-and-run style that can be played regardless of the market's condition, the trend, or the stock.

It shares some of the attributes of microtrading because the bulk of positions may be closed out in the same day. However, it also can be used to capture overnight gains in some situations. This leaves some flexibility for those who were always concerned about being too exposed to the market overnight.

Guerrilla trading is a unique style of play that is flexible and can often work best in the toughest markets.

> Guerrilla trading is a unique style of play that is flexible and can often work best in the toughest markets.

Self-test questions

1. In which type of market does guerrilla trading work best?

   a. A quiet or stable market.
   b. An upwardly trending market.
   c. A downwardly trending market.
   d. A choppy or uncertain market.

2. Guerrilla trades can be especially useful strategies because:

   a. They have a very high correlation to the overall market.
   b. They have a very low correlation to the overall market.
   c. Their correlation to the overall market varies.
   d. Their correlation to the overall market is irrelevant.

3. Your success as a guerrilla trader will depend most on what?

   a. Your ability to understand the emotional states of other market traders.
   b. Your ability to interpret a company's fundamentals.
   c. Your access to the opinions of leading stock analysts.
   d. The amount of inside information you can become privy to.

4. Why is the proper positioning of stops so important in guerrilla trading?

   a. Because every trade cannot be a winner.
   b. Because guerrilla trades often involve very large stock price moves.
   c. Because sound money-management is the key to making overall profits.
   d. All of the above.

5. Pristine Method strategies use charts to gauge the emotional state of the market over what time frame?

   a. Hourly.
   b. Daily.
   c. Monthly.
   d. Any time interval.

For answers, go to www.traderslibrary.com/TLEcorner

Chapter 2
The Tools for Guerrilla Trading

The tools for guerrilla trading are fairly simple. We need to become familiar with only three things in order to proceed. First, we need to have a basic understanding of Japanese candlesticks. All of my charts use Japanese candlesticks, no matter my style of trading.

Second, we need to look at one specific type of Japanese candlestick. It is known as the bullish or bearish 20/20 bar. This particular bar is common to all of the guerrilla tactics.

Last, we will discuss the concept of gaps in more detail. I ran over some basics in the previous chapter, but we will take a more detailed look. Gaps are required in some, but not all, of the guerrilla tactics.

The Japanese Candlestick

Technically, a Japanese candlestick does not display any more information than a regular bar chart. They both display the opening, closing, high, and low of a particular period. The difference is the Japanese candlesticks display the information in a way that is much easier to see visually. The area between the high low is colored either black or white, depending on whether the stock closed above or below its opening price. This places the emphasis on who won the battle each and every time period.

> Charts can be displayed in a line form, a bar form, or several other forms. The Japanese candlestick shows the information better visually than those other methods.

A good example of this difference in focus was seen on the day Microsoft gapped up $5. From the moment the stock opened, it began selling off and continued to drop steadily throughout the day until it had lost $3.50 of the morning gap. Late in the afternoon, the star of one of our favorite cable shows was giving her afternoon rundown and reported in an elated voice that, "Traders were buying up Microsoft all day long as the stock was trading $1.50 higher." While it is true that the stock was still up $1.50, the true sentiment of the stock was very bearish, as it had lost almost all of its opening gain.

This also allows for much more efficient scanning when looking for patterns. Take a look at the examples of these two Japanese candlesticks in Figure 2.1.

FIGURE 2.1- Determining Who Won the Battle

Determining Who Won The Battle

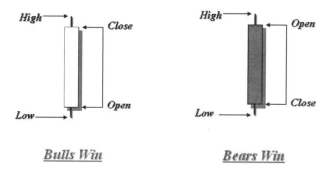

Bulls Win   Bears Win

For color charts go to www.traderslibrary.com/TLEcorner

Their black and white boxes represent the open and closing prices for that time. When the stock closes above its opening price, the bulls have won that session and the box is colored white. This is known as the body of the candlestick. The lines extending from the top and bottom of the body represent the high and low for that time period. These are called wicks, tails, or shadows. The second candle is black because the bears won the battle for this particular period of time. They were able to close the stock at the price at which it opened.

FIGURE 2.2- Bulls Win

Bulls Win

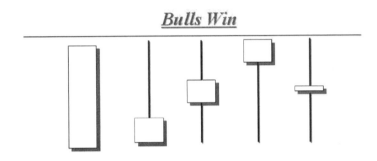

For color charts go to www.traderslibrary.com/TLEcorner

Figure 2.2 shows examples of five different bullish candles. They are all considered bullish because the body is white as the bulls closed the price above the opening price.

It is important to understand that while all of these candles are white, there is a great degree of difference in the bullishness of the candles. When the opening and closing price are very close together, the significance of black or white becomes less important. In these cases, the size and position of the tail becomes as important as the color of the candle.

In the examples above, the first and fourth candles are very bullish, not simply because of their white bars but because they closed at the high of the day's range. While the second candle is white, it can actually be considered somewhat of a bearish candle. This is because the white body is very small and there is a huge topping tail sitting on top of the body. This means that at one time, the bulls had run the stock all the way to the high of the day, as shown by the top of that topping tail. However, by the end of the day, the bears had run the stock down to near the low of the day. There is some truth in the old adage that novices open the market and professionals close the market.

> Topping tails and bottoming tails are the graffiti marks of big sellers and buyers and should be respected.

The Star Candle of Our Show- The 20/20 Bar

Let's move on to one specific type of Japanese candlestick known as the bullish or bearish 20/20 bar, shown in Figure 2.3. There are only two basic requirements for the formation of this bar. First, the bar must be above average in total length. Second, the tails of the bar must each comprise 20% or less of the total bar. This is where the name "20/20" comes from.

Naturally, when the bar is white, it is because it has managed to close above its opening price. This means the bulls have won the battle, so we call this bar a bullish 20/20 candlestick. It may be called a bull 20/20 for short, and you may see it abbreviated: + 20/20. Naturally, when the bar is black, it is because it has managed to close below its opening price. This means the bears have won the battle, so we call this bar a bearish 20/20 candlestick.

FIGURE 2.3- The 20/20 Candle

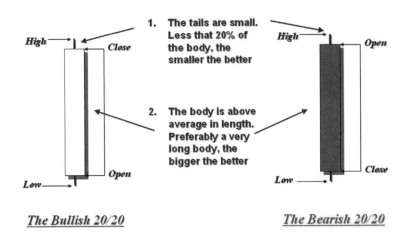

1. The tails are small. Less that 20% of the body, the smaller the better

2. The body is above average in length. Preferably a very long body, the bigger the better

The Bullish 20/20

The Bearish 20/20

For color charts go to www.traderslibrary.com/TLEcorner

Always Check the Charts

So there you have the technical requirements. At this point, you may be wondering things like, "How big is above average?" Often, when traders are learning technical patterns, they want very specific numbers as a guide. I could tell you that a 20/20 bar should be at least a $1.50 for an average $30 stock, but that would not be doing justice to the concept. You need to look to the entire picture.

For example, there was a time when Rambus (RMBS), a fast-moving high-tech stock, was the same price as Continental Airlines

(CAL), and they were both around $30. At that time, RMBS could move $1.50 in the first 10 minutes of trading. CAL would need the better part of a week to move the $1.50. So guidelines are guidelines, but the true picture comes from looking at the chart. What is an average move? How often does it happen?

> Determining the best 20/20 bar is really a visual concept. Guidelines may be used for the beginning trader; eventually, the pro must learn to recognize the moves that are important in the market.

Going beyond the technical requirements for the 20/20 bar, we must discuss another subject. While I have stated that the best of the guerrilla plays can be played in a vacuum, the real truth is that nothing is an absolute vacuum. Quality will vary in the guerrilla plays and, in some cases, the prior chart pattern may influence the overall trade. So let's talk about the emotions behind the 20/20 bar and why it works so well.

If the candle is white, greed is in play. If it's black, fear is in play. These are the dominant emotions. White means nothing more than the stock closed that bar higher than the open. If it's black, the stock closed that bar lower than the opening price. If the stock opens at 40 and closes at 42, we have a white bar. If the stock opens at 40 and closes at 38, we have a black bar. The opening price and the closing price are the two most important prices of the entire period.

The relationship of the open and close are the most important relationships, and the Japanese discovered this 1,000 years ago. It's really phenomenal. They rationalized that if the open and close are the two most important parts, why don't we accentuate that relationship by drawing a box around it? There it is. The white box represents the relationship between the open and close. The rest they called shadows, which means that they are important, but they are really only a slight reflection of the real part of the price.

The Bullish 20/20 Bar

But let's talk a little bit more about the bullish 20/20 bar. It's not just a white bar. It's a very long white bar that has the open at or near the low of the bar's range, and the close at or near the high of that bar's range.

What does it take to produce a bar that is not only white, but is bigger than most and has been dominated by the bulls the entire time? Buyers, and a lot of them. It takes a lot of greed. Once this bar has been formed, what do we know about all of the bullish traders at that moment? We know they have already jumped in. We know lots of bulls have bought lots of shares and have already committed to a long position in the stock.

> There are a finite number of bulls and bears on any particular stock. At some point, one or the other may run out.

Once this happens, we know two more pieces of information about the stock. First is the simple truth that if most of the bulls have already bought, there is very low buying power left to propel the stock higher. All the bullets have been fired. The second thing is that if this bar closes near the high, like all 20/20 bars must, we know it will not take much selling on the next bar to start producing pain for those who bought at the end of the big white bar. If those in pain begin to sell, the price drives lower and more bulls feel the pain. This can become a snowball effect.

So this event sets up what a lot of novice market players do not understand. They will look at that long, white bar and feel the need to jump on board. Sometimes this may be the correct action. Often, it is not. What makes the difference? What if the bullish 20/20 bar was following one or more prior white bars? What if it was follow-

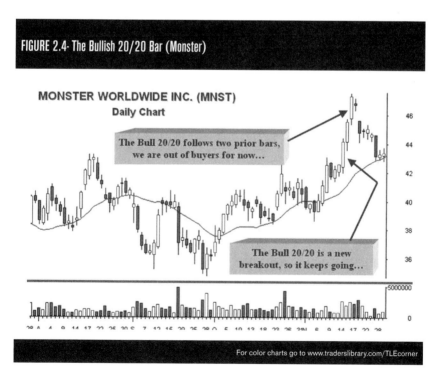

FIGURE 2.4- The Bullish 20/20 Bar (Monster)

MONSTER WORLDWIDE INC. (MNST)
Daily Chart

The Bull 20/20 follows two prior bars, we are out of buyers for now...

The Bull 20/20 is a new breakout, so it keeps going...

For color charts go to www.traderslibrary.com/TLEcorner

FIGURE 2.5- The Bullish 20/20 Bar (AKAMAI)

AKAMAI TECHNOLOGIES INC. (AKAM)
Daily Chart

The Bull 20/20 is a new breakout, so it keeps going...

For color charts go to www.traderslibrary.com/TLEcorner

ing five prior white bars? At some point, the assumption should be that the party is potentially close to over, at least short term.

On the other hand, if that bullish 20/20 bar was the very first white bar breaking out of a congested area, or reversing a prior downtrend, do you see how that new move may be more likely to attract additional buying? Figures 2.4 and 2.5 show you examples of 20/20 bars that create and end moves.

Remember that right now we are just looking at the formation of 20/20 bars. These are not strategies. There will be entry criteria for each play that must be met. That is why in Figure 2.5 you do not have to try to decide if the second white bar is a new or old move. It did not meet any entry criteria, so you would simply be watching it regardless of what opinion you had.

The Bearish 20/20 Bar

Now let's take a look at the bearish 20/20 bar concept. Naturally, like all things in trading, the bearish 20/20 is just the reverse of its bullish counterpart. We have a very long black bar with very small, if any, tails. This candle shows the bears have completely dominated the session.

If this is a daily chart, then the bears were in control the entire day. Fear was the dominating force. The stock opened at or near the high of the bar's range and it closed at or near the low of the bar's range, creating a nasty, long wide-range bar. The sellers have sold virtually all that they have of this stock. Individuals have already jumped off the ship; they've already waved their white flag.

So the trained trader sees a very long black bar. But, if it has followed one or more prior black bars, that trader begins to say, "Wait a minute," because the selling or a good portion of the selling has already happened.

Think about this as well. It is likely that if you turn on your favorite news show that discusses the stocks at the end of the day, the anchors will likely be talking about how negative this stock is and how bearish it was and how this stock has no future. The news usually does an excellent job getting the novice trader further on the wrong side of the play. By the time it's in the news, the play has already happened.

A trained technical trader never, ever, buys after a series of white bars. If there is one thing that you need to walk away with after reading this book, it is that a trained Pristine trader never buys greed. Trained traders buy after a series of black bars. That is buying after people have thrown in the white towel, after there is blood in the streets. That is when the trained trader steps up and says, "Sir, Madam, can I help you? Is that stock bothering you? I will take that off your hands if you like."

> The news usually does an excellent job helping novice traders get on the wrong side of the play.

And of course the reverse is also true. Do you know that this one rule can completely revolutionize your trading? Think about it. It may not make you a successful, profitable trader overnight. But I will guarantee you one thing: You will be buying more right, more often, than you will be buying wrong. We buy after pain and we sell after greed.

The Power of Gaps

Gaps in general can be the style of play that a trader may choose to use as a primary strategy. When gaps happen in such a way that they form one of these guerrilla tactics, they can be very powerful patterns.

When a gap occurs, it leaves what we call a "void" on the chart. If the stock gaps away from a prior price area, it leaves a visible white space on the chart. However, the stock can also gap in the other direction, into the prior price. This type of gap is not as obvious because it does not leave a white space on the chart. However, it is still a gap and still leaves a void for our purposes. The issue we are concerned about is that no trader is able to execute a trade in that void area. The best way to explain this is to put yourself on the wrong side of the gap and imagine the emotions you would be feeling.

> Many gaps can be played as strategies; but, when gaps occur in conjunction with the guerrilla pattern, a very powerful move can result.

Let's say you are a fairly new trader and you have found a stock that looks like it is going to move up. The strategy used, or whether it was even a good play, is not relevant. You enter the play and have a stop loss selected. You have taken a share size such that if the stock were to stop out, you would lose a fixed amount of money; let's say for the sake of this example, $1,000. Let's say you bought 1,000 shares of the stock at $32 and your protective stop loss was at $31. This is a swing or core trade (discussed in part three), so you are going to hold overnight.

Everything seems to be going fine until later that evening. The CEO of the company whose stock you just purchased holds a small press conference and announces that it appears they have some accounting irregularities. There may be an investigation forthcoming.

Whether you are a novice or a pro, you probably realize this news is not going to have a positive affect on your trading account. There is a rule among the trading gods that when you are new, any large gap must go against you. You may think the odds are 50-50, but it just doesn't work like that.

So how is all this going to play out the next morning? The market formally opens at 9:30 a.m. As many of you know, there is a pre-market session that begins at 8:00 a.m. While the market makers and specialists may not be participating, traders can trade during the pre- and post-market times. In either case, it is irrelevant in this scenario. The point is that when the first trade goes off, there will not be anybody there who wants to buy the stock at the price at which it closed the night before. Now remember, you bought the stock at $32 and your stop loss is at $31.

Let's say the stock did well the first day and closed at $33. Where is the stock going to open this morning? That will be up to the free and open market to decide. Nobody has to buy a stock at any price, but certainly there will be some price that will attract buyers. The only problem is that price may be far below where you purchased the stock and where you placed your stop loss.

So while the market is waiting to open, you see someone has entered a bid for your stock at $22. Wow, that can't be right, you think. But as market open draws nearer, you see nobody is topping that bid. So you decide to offer your stock at a loss at $30 to see if anyone will buy it. But there are no takers. So you drop to $29, and your stock just sits there. You notice now that somebody has increased the bid from $22 to $23, but still far from the price you want to get. You decide that $22 is too much of a loss to handle, so you're going to wait for the market to open and hope the stock makes a recovery.

So after all the jockeying between bids and offers, the stock finally opens at $23.50. It opened there because that is where there was the first meeting of minds between a buyer and seller. No one knows where the stock may go today, but someone was willing to bet that $23.50 was going to be the low, and someone else was happy to take that price. You quickly calculate that if you were to sell it at open, you would be down 7 1/2 times the amount of money you were allowed to lose. In your mind that is too much, so you hold on.

> No one is safe from the stock gapping against them if it is held overnight.

From the minute the stock opens, it continues to bleed down. It drops to $23, then to $22, and then seems to sit at $21. All during this bleed, there are traders in the same situation you are in. Every time the stock moves another penny down, another trader throws in the towel. As the stock breaks below $21, as painful as it is, you simply cannot afford to lose any more money. You now start to draw up images of the stock falling to $5—and what that would do to your trading account. So you sell.

I wish I could tell you it is uncommon for new traders to take large losses because they did not follow a stop loss. As you may guess, it is not. But notice there is a big difference here. You did not ignore your stop loss. There was a void between $33 and $23.50 where no one was allowed to trade the stock. The news made an immediate change in the stock price and the market opened at the new price. It did not matter if you were a professional trader or a novice. It did not matter if you always followed your stops. It did not matter if you had an automatic stop-loss program in your computer or sitting with your broker. All traders who were long the stock suffered that morning. That is what is so interesting about gaps.

I have walked you through a scenario so that you understand the emotions and how they play out when a gap occurs. In this particular case, a gap down made the stock a loser. Sometimes a similar situation can happen, but because of a different chart pattern, the gap down makes the stock rally. This is what guerrilla trading is all about.

1. The charts used for guerrilla trading analysis are generally:

   a. Point-and-figure charts.

   b. Open-high-low-close bar charts.

   c. Japanese candlestick charts.

   d. Simple line charts.

2. When reviewing a candlestick chart, a white box indicates the stock being analyzed:

   a. Closed unchanged.

   b. Closed above its opening price.

   c. Closed below its opening price.

   d. Opened above its prior-day closing price.

3. In a Japanese candlestick chart, the line extending above or below the "body" of the candlestick is called:

   a. A wick.

   b. A tail.

   c. A shadow.

   d. All of the above names are used to describe this feature.

4. The most important bar to look for in analyzing a chart for guerrilla trading is:

   a. The bullish or bearish 20/20 bar.
   b. The 10-minute reversal bar.
   c. A bullish bar with a tail longer than the body.
   d. A bullish or bearish 30/30 bar.

5. A bar with a very long black body and short tails shows the analyst that:

   a. Greed was the dominating force in the market that day.
   b. The bulls were in control of the market that day.
   c. The bears were in control of the market that day.
   d. The market was generally stable with little change in price.

For answers, go to www.traderslibrary.com/TLEcorner

Chapter 3

Gap and Snap and Gap and Crap Plays

The Pristine Gap and Snap

Now that we have an understanding of the tools we need for guerrilla trading, let's take a look at our first tactic, one of my favorites. It's called the Pristine Gap and Snap Play, and it happens every single day in the market. This method works best as a one- to two-day trading tactic on volatile NASDAQ stocks above $35 per share. That doesn't mean you cannot use guerrilla tactics on anything else; it simply means that this is where they work best.

The Setup

Let's go over the setup in Figure 3.1. We need two black bars in a row and the second bar must be a bearish 20/20 bar.

FIGURE 3.1- Pristine Snap n Gap Tactic One (The Set-up)

The Setup / The Action

1. **The stock should be down at least two days in a row.**

2. **We need a wide-range bar on the current day. At least $1.50 point.**

3. **The open of the current day must be in the top 20% of the day's price range.**

4. **The close must be in the bottom 20% of the day's price range.**

Stock down 2 days in a row.

For color charts go to www.traderslibrary.com/TLEcorner

For that second bar to be a bearish 20/20 bar, we want it to be an extra wide bar with little or no tails. Again, a general rule of thumb would be $1.50 in length for an average $30 stock, with the tails less than 20% of the total body.

If we have more than two bars down, that is even better. The more the merrier. The concept here is we want an overdone condition. We need a minimum of two days of pain, and with the last day being the 20/20 bar, we know most of the pain is coming at the end of the move. That is what we want to see.

The Action

Once this setup occurs, we need to have the stock gap down by at least 50 cents on the next day. This is the only way we can have an actionable event for this strategy. If we have the stock gapping down, there will be a void in the chart between the current day's opening price and the prior day's closing price. If the stock can rally to fill that void, we are going to strike by buying the stock 5 to 10 cents above the low of the prior bar.

Here is the rationale for the Gap and Snap Play (Figure 3.2). We have a situation in which the stock has been in pain for a period

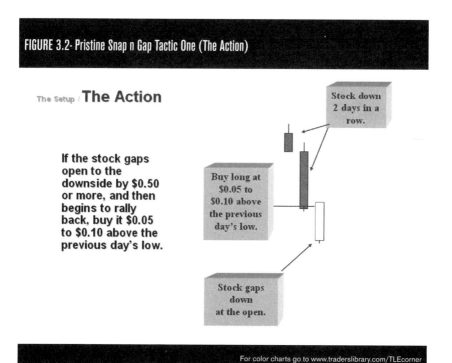

FIGURE 3.2- Pristine Snap n Gap Tactic One (The Action)

The Setup / **The Action**

If the stock gaps open to the downside by $0.50 or more, and then begins to rally back, buy it $0.05 to $0.10 above the previous day's low.

Buy long at $0.05 to $0.10 above the previous day's low.

Stock down 2 days in a row.

Stock gaps down at the open.

of time. The pain has accelerated the last day, as we can see by the bearish 20/20 bar. As the typical investors come home from work and check their stock, they find that what had been painful has just become desperately painful—their stock just had the biggest decrease since they purchased it. They instruct their broker to sell the stock the next morning. Without any further instructions, this becomes an order to sell at the open.

> When possible, we want to be on the side of the market maker.

When market makers receive enough of these orders to sell at the open, it becomes a situation they can take advantage of. You see, their job is to be the buyer of last resort. So, if a flood of sell orders comes in and the market makers are forced to be the buyer, where do you think they want to purchase the stock? They will try to make sure the stock opens as low as possible. Often, this extra move down sets the low as professionals come in to buy the oversold condition.

The question will always be whether this stock will continue lower after the gap down. That is why we have the entry requirement for this stock. We do not buy at the open. We also do not buy it after a casual move up. Many novices will buy anything that gaps down, assuming that all gaps must be filled. What we want to see is enough strength continuing to come into the stock that, even after it fills the gap, it is able to continue climbing higher. Then we will have a good indication that we have professional players buying the stock.

The Setup / **The Action**

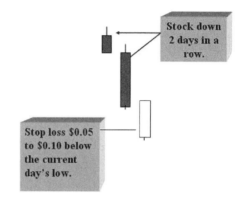

Place a protective stop $0.05 to $0.10 below the current day's low.

Stock down 2 days in a row.

Sell for a $2 plus profit or on the 2nd day, whichever comes first.

Stop loss $0.05 to $0.10 below the current day's low.

For color charts go to www.traderslibrary.com/TLEcorner

Immediately after buying the stock, we need to take out our insurance policy. It does not matter how accurate you feel a strategy is, or how safe you feel a particular play is. Trades can go against you and you need to limit your loss on the downside. For this strategy, we place our protective stop loss 5 to 10 cents under the current day's bar (Figure 3.3).

Remember, it only takes one missed stop to create a serious dent in your trading capital. Always place your protective stop loss after entering the play.

Next is our target area. As I mentioned earlier, the target areas for guerrilla plays are not as exact as some of our other strategies. For an average $30 stock, we are going to be looking for a $2 profit, or to sell no later than the morning of the third day, whichever comes first. If, on the third day, we have not met our profit objective, we sell it. So we will either get stopped out, get our $2 profit, or sell on the third day, no exceptions.

Every single trade you take, no matter what the strategy, must have four clearly defined parts. They are: 1) the entry; 2) the protective stop; 3) the target; and 4) the management system (more on this in part three). For this Gap and Snap Play, I have outlined each of these for you. The management system is what we call all-or-nothing. We either reach our target or get stopped out.

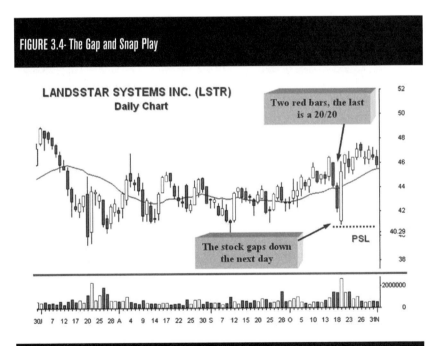

FIGURE 3.4- The Gap and Snap Play

Figure 3.4 is an example of a Gap and Snap Play. We have our two days down, and the second bar is a bearish 20/20 bar. The stock gaps down a significant amount, so we will be entering 5 to 10 cents above the low of the prior day. Our protective stop loss is set under the current day's low, and, in this case, our target objective is easily met in one day.

The Pristine Gap and Crap

Now it is time to teach the counterpart, the bearish version of this play. It is known as the Pristine Gap and Crap Play.

FIGURE 3.5- The Pristine Gap n Crap/ Tactic Two – Setup

The Setup / The Action

1. **The stock should be up at least two days in a row.**

2. **Wide-range day at least $1.75 point.**

3. **The open must be in the low 20% of the day's range.**

4. **The close must be in the high 20% of the day's range.**

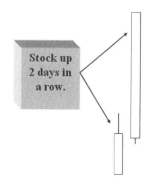

Stock up 2 days in a row.

The Setup

The setup for the Gap and Crap Play (Figure 3.5) is two white bars with the second bar being a bullish 20/20 bar.

Again, it is critical that the second bar be an extra wide bar with little or no tails. Notice that I have identified the guideline on this play to be a wide bar of $1.75 or more. I have found that the short version of the strategy works better if that 20/20 bar is extra long.

If there are two, three, four or more white bars, then it is even better. The idea is that we want to see greed overdone. The minimum, however, is two.

FIGURE 3.6- The Pristine Gap n Crap/ Tactic 2 – Action

The Setup / **The Action**

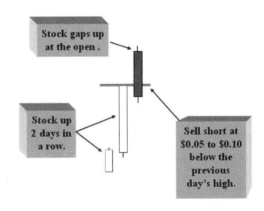

If the stock gaps open to the upside by $0.50 or more, and then begins to fall back, sell (short) $0.05 to $0.10 below the previous day's high.

Stock gaps up at the open.

Stock up 2 days in a row.

Sell short at $0.05 to $0.10 below the previous day's high.

The Action

Once you find this setup, you put it on your watch list for the next day. You'll be looking for this stock to gap up 50 cents or more (Figure 3.6). If it does not gap up, it is not meeting the criteria for this play. Since the stock is gapping up and away from a prior white bar, there will be a noticeable void on the chart. If the stock begins to sell off, our action is to short the stock 5 to 10 cents below the high of the bullish 20/20 bar.

Here is what is happening if the market gaps up and forms a Gap and Crap Play: We know the vast majority of the public will not enter a long position until it has proven itself by trading up for a significant period of time. Even though the stock has traded for two or more days, the bullish 20/20 bar is proof to some people this stock should now be played long.

Again, the typical trader leaves for work and decides it is time to get some of this hot-moving stock. He leaves instructions with the broker to buy the stock at open. When several of these orders come in, the market maker again has a type of blank check. If a lot of people want to buy and there are no sellers available, he is a seller of last resort. But since there are no sellers available, he can pretty much set the price at which the stock will open.

So, now we have a similar question. If the market maker knows he has to sell this stock to the public, and he can choose his price, would he prefer to open the stock as high as possible or at yesterday's close? The gap in the stock is a gift to the bulls and causes traders who are currently long the stock to take their profits—and a selling spree begins. Remember, the market maker who sold short at the open is making money during this entire decline. We want to be side-by-side with the market maker and enjoying the decline in the stock.

To ensure this is really what is occurring, we do not randomly short the stock at open. We wait to make sure the weakness is more than just some casual selling. Our signal is when the stock is able to trade below the prior day's high.

As always, immediately after short selling this stock, we place our protective stop loss over the high of the current day (Figure 3.7).

FIGURE 3.7- Pristine Gap n Crap/ Tactic 2 – Action, Place a Protective Stop

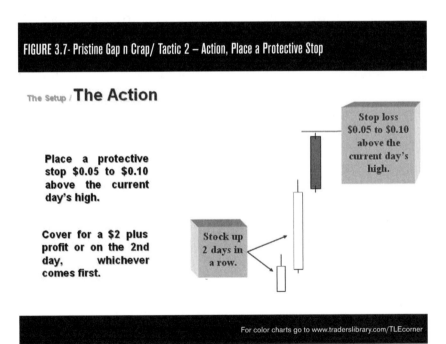

The Setup / **The Action**

Place a protective stop $0.05 to $0.10 above the current day's high.

Cover for a $2 plus profit or on the 2nd day, whichever comes first.

Stock up 2 days in a row.

Stop loss $0.05 to $0.10 above the current day's high.

For color charts go to www.traderslibrary.com/TLEcorner

From here forward, I am simply going to talk about buying or selling above or below a certain point. I am not going to continue to repeat the part about adding 5 to 10 cents to the entry. The reason we use an additional 5 to 10 cents is to avoid what we call a "false trigger."

Very simply, it is easy for a stock to trade 1 or 2 pennies above or below any area at any time. It was not long ago that the smallest increment a stock could move was a "teenie," which meant 1/16th of the dollar. That was when the market traded in fractions. Today, with many stocks trading at a 1 penny level, false triggers are much more common.

FIGURE 3.8- The Gap n Crap Play (BAIDU)

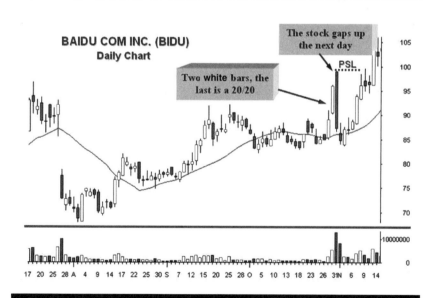

Gap and Snap and Gap and Crap Plays | 39

For our target area, we will be looking for the stock to drop at least $2 for an average $30 stock, but not any longer than the morning of the third day.

Note that there are variations you can use for your profit-taking. I am a big believer in selling incrementally. You may want to revise your target-taking strategy to take profits on part of the position at the close of first day, especially if you are holding a large share size for an overnight position.

In Figure 3.8, we see an example of a Gap and Crap Play. It is an interesting chart because it goes against what many novice traders might do. The stock is up for two solid days, and we have a perfect bullish 20/20 bar the prior day. This does appear to be a fairly bullish breakout on this chart, but the 20/20 bar is extra-large and the gap up is also extreme. This simply caused extreme profit-taking. That is what we're looking for on the guerrilla plays, one- to two-day hits.

1. Some of the most rewarding guerrilla tactics involve searching for gaps that can most often be identified on what type of charts?

   a. Two-minute charts.
   b. Hourly charts.
   c. Daily charts.
   d. Weekly charts.

2. The setup for a Pristine Gap and Snap play requires what?

   a. A minimum of two consecutive black bars, the final one being a bearish 20/20 bar.
   b. A minimum of two consecutive white bars, the second with a longer body than the first.
   c. At least two alternating black and white bars, with the second longer than the first.
   d. Two black or two white bars of approximately the same length.

3. When a stock gaps lower at the opening, then rebounds through the gap, it is a good sign that:

   a. Novices have rushed into the market and are likely heading for a fall.
   b. The stock will resume its downward trend later in the trading session.
   c. Professional players have entered the market, giving the stock enough strength to continue its rebound.
   d. The market for this stock is mixed and it's impossible to tell which way it will move next.

4. When you do a Gap and Snap Play, buying a stock at around $30 a share, you should:

   a. Immediately set a stop loss $0.05 to $0.10 below the current day's low.
   b. Set a target profit of $2.00 or more and sell as soon as it's achieved.
   c. Plan to take sell on the second market day if neither the stop nor the target is hit.
   d. All of the above.

5. Entry to the Pristine Gap and Crap play requires that a stock:

    a. Close lower for two or more consecutive days, then close higher for a full session.

    b. Close higher for two or more consecutive days, gap higher at the opening the next morning, then reverse and move below the prior day's high.

    c. Move lower for three consecutive days, then gap higher at the opening the next day, penetrating the prior day's low.

    d. Trade flat for two or more consecutive days, then gap either higher or lower at the opening the next day.

For answers, go to www.traderslibrary.com/TLEcorner

Chapter 4

Gap Surprise Plays

Let's move on to our second set of tactics, the Gap Surprise plays. The good news is we have a very similar setup to what was required for our first two tactics. There will simply be a different event and emotional state that causes the action. First, I am going to review the Pristine Bullish Gap Surprise Play. This method works best as a one- to two-day trading tactic and on volatile NASDAQ stocks above $35. Again, this tactic can be used on other stocks; these are just the best.

The Bullish Gap Surprise Setup

For our setup, we're going to require at least two black bars, with the second bar being a bearish 20/20 bar. In addition, we want to make sure we have all above-average or climactic volume on the

FIGURE 4.1- Bullish Gap Surprise – Tactic Three/ Setup

The Setup / The Action

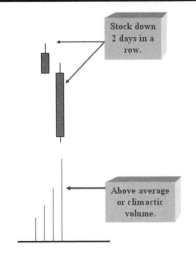

1. The stock should be down at least two days in a row.

2. We need a wide-range day of at least $1.75 point.

3. The open must be in the top 20% of the day's range.

4. The close must be in the bottom 20% of the day's range.

5. Above average volume on the current day (preferably climactic volume).

bearish 20/20 bar. There is a very good reason for this; you will see when we get into the psychology of this play.

Let's start by defining "above average volume" and "climactic volume." When the volume of the current candle is greater than the volume of the prior five candles, I consider that above-average. When the volume of the current candle is more than twice the average of the last couple of weeks, I consider that climactic. For this strategy, we need above-average volume at a minimum. Climactic is even better.

The Action

Once you find this setup on your nightly scans, you put it on your watch list for the next day. This time we will be monitoring to see if the stock gaps up significantly. Notice that this type will be gapping back into the prior bar rather than creating a white spot on the chart. If we do have the stock gapping at least 50 cents for an average $30 stock, our strategy is to buy the stock immediately after open. A more conservative entry would be to wait for 5 minutes and only buy if the stock trades above the high created during the first 5 minutes. This is known as buying the 5-minute high.

FIGURE 4.2- Bullish Gap Surprise – Tactic Three/ Action

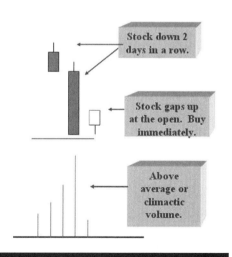

The Setup / **The Action**

If the stock opens (gaps) up by at least $0.50 above the previous day's closing price, *buy it immediately*. You can also buy it above the first 5 min. high (Conservative).

Stock down 2 days in a row.

Stock gaps up at the open. Buy immediately.

Above average or climactic volume.

For color charts go to www.traderslibrary.com/TLEcorner

A couple words about each of these entries. I've called the 5-minute high entry a more conservative entry. The reason is that if you play the stock immediately at open, you'll be involved in a higher percentage of stop outs. It is only common sense. While this is a very powerful play, you will naturally avoid some stop outs if you let the stock trade for 5 minutes, since many of the failures occur immediately at the open.

So why not wait for 5 minutes on every play? When these Bullish Gap Surprises work well, they often move a great distance, even in 5 minutes. On some plays, you may be giving up a significant part of your profit by waiting too long for the entry. This issue of deciding between a more assured entry with less profit versus a lower odds entry with higher profit is one that you always face in trading. The decision comes down to your temperament and trading style.

One other comment: If you are going to play the immediate entry, the word immediate includes delaying a few seconds to make sure the stock is trading in the direction you desire. It is not uncommon when a stock gaps for it to open exactly at its high or low for the day and then never return to that area. If you are playing long, you don't want to buy the high of the day to the penny and watch the stock fall all day.

> There are always trade-offs in trading. Quicker entries are best when you are right, but will also suffer the greatest failure rate. You must decide how aggressive or conservative your trading style will be.

The reason a Bullish Gap Surprise Play can work so well is because of what we call shock value. When a stock closes very weak and in a downtrend, as this setup requires, it is not uncommon for the stock to continue down. As a matter of fact, many traders may take positions in the latter part of the day by shorting the stock, expecting the stock to continue or to gap down the next day. Also, anyone already in the stock as a short position should feel very comfortable holding overnight because the stock closed at the low of the day.

Now the Surprise

All of those who shorted at the end the day expecting a quick move down are now under water. Those who have been holding the stock are seeing their profit dwindle and will decide it's time to take the money and run. Once the stock starts moving up, there may be traders waiting to be long on the stock because of its oversold condition. The reason we like to see increased volume on the last day down is because it shows that we have a large new pool of people who just sold the stock. These are all potential longs the next day when the stock gaps up.

Immediately after buying the stock, we need to place our protective stop loss under the low of the prior day. Figure 4.3 illustrates the situation further.

There's really no other option in this case. Today's low will always be higher than the prior day because we have just gapped up by definition. It is only if you wait for the 5-minute high that today's

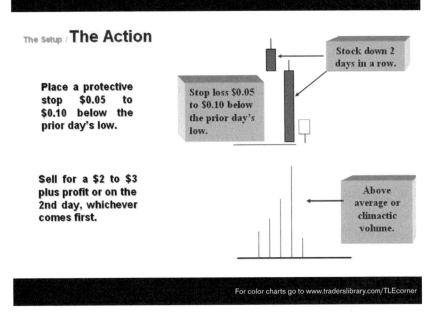

The Setup / **The Action**

Place a protective stop $0.05 to $0.10 below the prior day's low.

Stop loss $0.05 to $0.10 below the prior day's low.

Stock down 2 days in a row.

Sell for a $2 to $3 plus profit or on the 2nd day, whichever comes first.

Above average or climactic volume.

For color charts go to www.traderslibrary.com/TLEcorner

low could possibly be lower than yesterday's low. If that is the case, then use today's low. When buying an immediate entry, it is generally not wise to use today's low because it will be a penny or two under where you buy the stock if you buy immediately, and would be highly likely to stop out quickly.

An example of a Bullish Gap Surprise is shown in Figure 4.4. The stock was going along in a nice uptrend when a big black bar developed. Notice this bar occurred after the stock had gapped up after five white bars. Does this sound familiar? This is not the official Gap and Crap Play because there was no 20/20 bar involved. However, in this case, the effect was similar. A second bearish 20/20

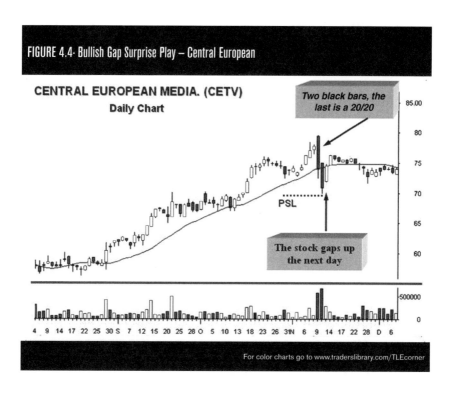

FIGURE 4.4- Bullish Gap Surprise Play – Central European

CENTRAL EUROPEAN MEDIA. (CETV)
Daily Chart

Two black bars, the last is a 20/20

PSL

The stock gaps up the next day

For color charts go to www.traderslibrary.com/TLEcorner

bar then developed and the next day the stock gapped up. Notice how the stock basically opened on its low that day and traded straight up for two days. Also notice the huge volume on the bearish 20/20 bar.

The Bearish Gap Surprise Setup

The setup for the Bearish Gap Surprise Play (Figure 4.5) requires two white bars, with the second white bar being a bullish 20/20 bar. Again, just like its counterpart, we want to see at least increased volume on the bullish 20/20 day.

FIGURE 4.5- Bearish Gap Surprise – Tactic Four

The Setup / The Action

1. The stock should be up at least two days in a row.

2. We need a wide-range day of at least $1.75 point.

3. The open must be in the bottom 20% of the day's range.

4. The close must be in the top 20% of the day's range.

5. Above average volume on the current day (preferably climactic volume).

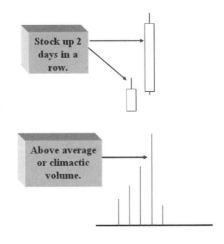

Stock up 2 days in a row.

Above average or climactic volume.

For color charts go to www.traderslibrary.com/TLEcorner

For all of these 20/20 bars, the general rule is the bigger the better. If this Bearish Gap Surprise setup has a huge white bar with no tails on climactic volume, it is the ideal play. If it is up several days instead of two, that makes it all the better. Let's take a look at what happens when this play hits.

The Action

While monitoring this strategy for an entry, we are naturally looking for a bearish gap down. Remember as a guideline that it should be at least 50 cents for a $30 stock. Remember, also, the true

FIGURE 4.6- Bearish Gap Surprise – Tactic Four/ The Action

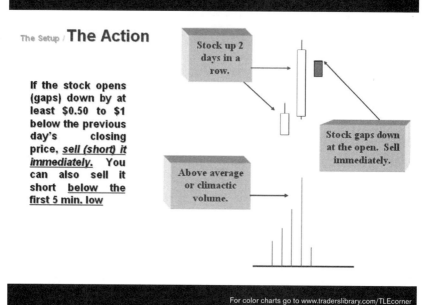

The Setup / **The Action**

If the stock opens (gaps) down by at least $0.50 to $1 below the previous day's closing price, _sell (short) it immediately._ You can also sell it short _below the first 5 min. low_

Stock up 2 days in a row.

Stock gaps down at the open. Sell immediately.

Above average or climactic volume.

guide is a visual look at the chart at the time the gap hits. Review Figure 4.6.

Once we have this setup, if the stock gaps down a significant amount, we want to short the stock immediately. A more conservative approach would be to wait to short the 5-minute low. All of the comments regarding the immediate entry verses the 5-minute entry from the prior section (Bullish Gap Surprise) still apply. If you do wait for the 5-minute entry, it is possible that it may not occur until much later in the day. This is perfectly fine, and as a matter of fact, it is more likely to be a true multi-day move if the selling comes at the end of the day rather than the beginning.

One other thought on the topic of entries. If torn between the immediate entry and the 5-minute entry, I sometimes will make the decision based on the general market environment. If we are in a very bullish market environment, I would be more likely to play the Bullish Gap Surprise with an immediate entry and wait for the 5-minute rule on the Bearish Gap Surprise. The end result of the guerrilla tactic may not be affected much by the market, but the preliminary reaction, at the time the shock hits the open, may be influenced by an initial tendency to follow the mood of the market.

As always, once we're in the play, all our attention should turn to making sure our protective stop loss is in place. The same

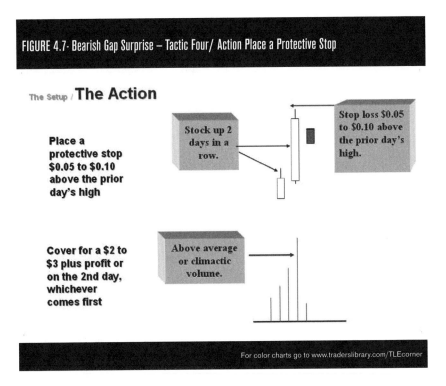

FIGURE 4.7- Bearish Gap Surprise – Tactic Four/ Action Place a Protective Stop

stop strategy is employed by both of the Gap Surprise strategies (Figure 4.7).

Our stop goes over the high of the prior day's bar. That would be the height of the bullish 20/20 bar. Remember the theory here. It is the initial shock of the gap down that should drive the stock lower. Sometimes it may consolidate near its opening price or slightly below, but if the stock is able to rally to above the prior day, the driving force of this play is gone.

> When a guerrilla play goes bad, it may be very bad; so be sure to always use your protective stop loss.

As you know, most traders fail at trading because of the inability to adhere to their protective stop loss. You need to make sure you honor your stop losses, as guerrilla trading is no place to begin experimenting. These patterns are usually going to move; and, if we are wrong, we are usually dead wrong. If you hold one that goes against you, it may become quite painful. When a good strategy does fail, the move in the other direction is often extreme. Don't be caught on the wrong end of one of these plays—use your stop loss.

Here in Figure 4.8 is an example of a Bearish Gap Surprise that occurred on Novelus Systems Inc. (NVLS).

The stock had been up for four days in a row, and the fourth day was an exceptionally long bullish 20/20 bar. The gap down was also extreme, as it opened at a price that erased three-fourths of the prior day's gains. Gaps like this often set long-term tops or bottoms in

FIGURE 4.8- Bullish Gap Surprise Play/ Novelus

NOVELUS SYS INC. (NVLS)
Daily Chart

Two green bars, the last is a 20/20

PSL

The stock gaps down the next day

For color charts go to www.traderslibrary.com/TLEcorner

the stock. In this case the stock fell nicely over the next three days for a gain, even though it came up short of the $2 target.

Here are my final thoughts on the Gap Surprise plays (which are among my favorites) before moving on to our next strategy. The performance of these plays will vary directly with the quality of the 20/20 bar and the size of a gap. There is a Catch-22 here that makes some of these plays difficult for the novice trader to take. The fact of the matter is that the bigger the gap, the more likely the play is to be successful. However, there is a tendency among traders to not take these plays because the stock appears extended at the time of the gap.

> It is always the case that the best plays are the ones that aren't apparent to the average person. It is the disbelief that eventually makes the play work.

However, the term "extended" can be quite an ambiguous and even dangerous term in trading. When a stock gaps up a significant amount, you may hear a financial commentator say the stock is now "too extended" to buy. This is because he is looking at fundamentals and using various accounting numbers that involve the price of the stock.

Just as an example, if the stock were to gap up 10%, its P/E (price-to-earnings) ratio would also go up 10% because he uses the price of the stock in the numerator of the calculation. The P/E ratio is a fundamental type of number.

From a technical point of view, the above argument is senseless. How many people actually bought the stock during that 10% move? The answer is not one. Not a single person was able to purchase stock at any price in between the original price and the 10% higher price. This means that 100% of the potential buyers still need to buy the stock. Whether they are covering short positions, or whether the stock has now made a move that justifies it as a long position, the only price for entry is here, now, at the new price. That makes it a little difficult to call the stock "extended" in my view.

Self-test questions

1. The Pristine Bullish Gap Surprise Play works best:

   a. As a three- to four-day trading tactic.
   b. On volatile NASDAQ stocks priced at or above $35 per share.
   c. On stable Blue Chip stocks paying sizable dividends.
   d. As a medium-term play to capture a reversal in an upwardly trending stock.

2. In the setup for a Bullish Gap Surprise Play, the chart must show at least two black bars, the second being a bearish 20/20 bar established on:

   a. Underlying bullish sentiment.
   b. Below-average volume.
   c. Above-average volume.
   d. A very narrow trading range.

3. When you find a setup for a Bullish Gap Surprise Play, you put it on your watch list for the next day and monitor looking for what?

   a. A continuation of the bearish move at the open.
   b. A downward gap opening of at least 75 cents for a $30 stock.
   c. An upward gap opening of at least 50 cents for a $30 stock.
   d. An opening price unchanged from the prior day's close.

4. A more conservative approach to entering a Gap Surprise Play involves waiting how long after the opening before taking action?

   a. Five minutes.
   b. Thirty minutes.
   c. One hour.
   d. Until the opening market report on CNN.

5. Sometimes, the best approach to entering Bullish or Bearish Gap Surprise Plays is to act:

   a. Only when the play is counter to the prevailing market trend.
   b. Only when the play goes in the direction of the prevailing market trend.
   c. Only when the market is choppy and there's no defined trend.
   d. Only on days when major economic reports are due.

For answers, go to www.traderslibrary.com/TLEcorner

Chapter 5

Bullish and Bearish 20/20 Plays

The Bullish 20/20

It is now time to learn our fifth and sixth tactics, known as the Bullish 20/20 and Bearish 20/20 plays. These are the third pair of tactics that will use a setup very similar to what we have seen so far. I will begin with the Bullish 20/20 Play. Like the others, this tactic works best as a one- to two-day trading tactic and on volatile NASDAQ stocks above $35.

The Setup

The setup for the Bullish 20/20 Play (Figure 5.1) is going to be almost identical to the setup for the Bullish Gap Surprise.

FIGURE 5.1- Bullish 20/20 Play – Tactic Five

The Setup / The Action

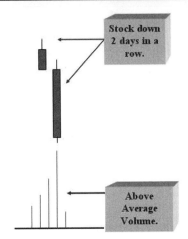

Stock down 2 days in a row.

Above Average Volume.

1. The stock should be down at least two days in a row.

2. We need a wide-range day of at least $1.75 point.

3. The open must be in the top 20% of the day's range.

4. The close must be in the bottom 20% of the day's range.

5. Above average volume on the current day (optional).

For color charts go to www.traderslibrary.com/TLEcorner

The only difference is going to be that the increase in volume is optional on this play; it is required on the Bullish Gap Surprise. I want to point out a tip when using the Bullish 20/20 play. You are about to see that the action required for this play is very passive. The prior plays had a gap occurring that can cause immediate movement in the stock. Because this play does not have that, I really like to see stock more than two days down when possible. This play relies on the fact that we have bled out the sellers more than on the other plays.

The Action

For the Gap Surprise plays, we gapped into the prior bars, going against the trend of the prior two days. For the Gap and Snap or Gap and Crap plays, we gapped away from the prior bars, going in the same direction as the trend of the prior two days. As you may have guessed by now, this play will handle what happens when the stock does not gap.

For the purpose of this play, anything that was not a gap up or a gap down under the prior definitions is now going to be considered a neutral opening and will qualify for the Bullish 20/20 play. We will be playing the stock long against the trend of the prior two

FIGURE 5.2- Bullish 20/20 Play – Tactic Five/ The Action

The Setup / **The Action**

If the stock opens less then $0.50 above or below the previous day's low, wait for 30 minutes of trading to transpire. Then, *buy* the stock an $0.05 to $0.10 above the high established during the first 30 minutes of trading.

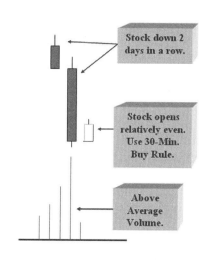

Stock down 2 days in a row.

Stock opens relatively even. Use 30-Min. Buy Rule.

Above Average Volume.

days, but only if the stock can prove it has the strength to trade above its 30-minute high (Figure 5.2).

This is why I cautioned to make sure you have an excellent setup for this play. The action for the other setups requires a gap, and a gap has some intrinsic value the moment it happens. If the stock opens neutral, we need to make sure the bearishness of the prior days is overcome. While it is not a guarantee, generally stocks do not trade above the 30-minute high unless they are done falling. That is the entry criteria for this play. Wait a full 30 minutes, mark off the high of the day, and enter long only if the stock trades over that 30-minute high.

I want to go over some of the exact details about using a 30-minute high. It seems pretty straightforward, but there are some nuances to learn that can save you money if you understand them. The general concept is that we want to see a show of strength. We want to see a stock that has rallied, declined, and then has finally decided to trade higher.

Be careful of some of the entries that may trick you. The first one is the stock that just continues to grind up for 30 straight minutes. If the stock has been continuously moving up for 30 minutes and then makes a new high shortly after 10:00 a.m., this is not the 30-minute high I want to take. There is nothing magical about the clock striking 10:00 a.m. Stocks actually tend to reverse at 10:00, so if the move has been up for 30-minutes, it will likely pull back. If this occurs, wait for the stock to pull back, even if it takes longer than 30 minutes, and then use the 30-minute high for the entry.

> Note that this play has the most conservative entry, the 30-minute high. Do not try to change that. This play requires this type of entry because there is no gap to ignite the play.

The other potential danger is entering a 30-minute high that is simply too extended based on the move that occurred since the stock opened. I am using that forbidden word "extended" because I have no other quick guideline to give you without getting into a whole other chapter about trading. I think you get the point though, that there is a limit to how far you can chase the stock, even on a guerrilla tactic.

As we must do for every trade we take, let's discuss the protective stop loss. For the first two strategies there was really no option as to where to put the stop.

This is the first time that we actually have two different bars that could be used for the stop. We are going to set our stop to the low of the current bar or the prior bar, whichever is lower (Figure 5.3). Very often, these two bars will have very similar lows. That is because we know for this strategy that the stock did not gap, so it must be opening in the general vicinity of the prior day's close. The only time today's bar will be significantly lower than the prior bar is when the stock initially sells off and then returns with strength later in the day. If the stock has rallied so far during 30 minutes and the stock is going to be excessively far away, it is usually best to pass the trade. This is the situation I discussed above when talking about how to handle various 30-minute entries.

The Setup / **The Action**

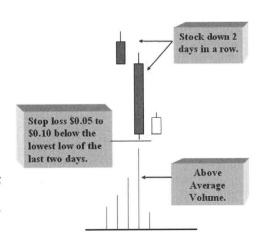

Place a protective stop $0.05 to $0.10 below the current day's low or the previous day's low, *whichever is lower*.

Sell for a $2 plus profit or on the 2nd day, whichever comes first.

Stop loss $0.05 to $0.10 below the lowest low of the last two days.

Stock down 2 days in a row.

Above Average Volume.

For color charts go to www.traderslibrary.com/TLEcorner

Our target will be the same as with the prior strategies. We expect to see a $2 or more profit for an average $30 stock and we want to be out of the stock by the second day, or no later than the morning of the third. Remember, these are quick hits. We are often planning against the dominant trend because of the particular situation that is set up as a guerrilla tactic. If the stock is not moving significantly in the first couple of days, it is likely that it will resume its original move; so it is best to get out. In Figure 5.4 we see an example of the Bullish 20/20 play on the stock Nutri Systems, Inc. (NTRI).

In the middle of the chart, we see a three-bar drop that ended with a very nice bearish 20/20 bar. This bar also came on increased

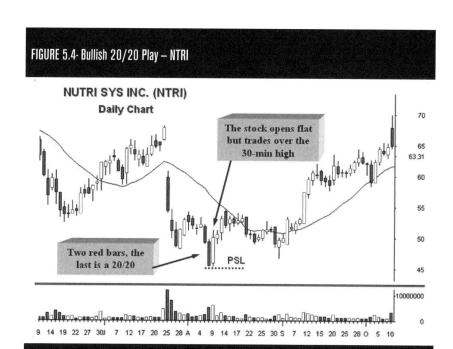

FIGURE 5.4- Bullish 20/20 Play – NTRI

NUTRI SYS INC. (NTRI)
Daily Chart

The stock opens flat but trades over the 30-min high

Two red bars, the last is a 20/20

PSL

For color charts go to www.traderslibrary.com/TLEcorner

volume. While this is optional for this play, it is always very nice to see the increased volume on the last day down. The next day, NTRI reversed direction and eventually traded through the entire bearish 20/20 bar. That is actually a second guerrilla tactic that was triggered.

If you only have the daily chart available to you, you have to make an assumption here. We technically don't know when the 30-minute high occurred, and we are actually not even sure this play would have been entered. It is possible, though not likely, that the stock ran and made its high of the day during the first 30 minutes. If that happened, there never would have been an entry. A very high percentage of the time, stocks in this situation first trade down to check the prior day's low before moving up. That is what likely caused the small bottoming tail on the current day's bar.

Even though it was after the fact, I want you to notice the overall pattern that formed here. Between the bearish 20/20 bar and the current day bar, the stock completely reversed direction and did so on very high volume. This type of pattern often makes a long term bottom on the daily chart.

The Bullish 20/20 play is probably the most common guerrilla tactic. You'll find a lot of these. Any time a stock has a sell-off, as long as there is a prior day decline, it will qualify for the setup. Since we do not need a gap, most stocks will be eligible candidates for entries on the 30-minute high on the following day.

Whenever you have a variety of places to choose from, it is always prudent to tighten your standards and look for the best possible setups. The best Bullish 20/20 plays will be found if you remember to look for the widest 20/20 bars that have occurred on increased volume after several days down.

Bearish 20/20 Play

It is time to review the Bearish 20/20 Play. It is true that with most every tactic in trading, the long and short version of any play will be identical. The same is true with the guerrilla tactics. As we have been reviewing the short versions of each play, I have been bringing out additional tidbits of information. The Bearish 20/20 play is very straightforward, and it is the last strategy that uses this basic two-bar setup we have been discussing. Like the others, this tactic works best as a one- to two-day trading tactic on volatile NASDAQ stocks above $35.

The Setup

Figure 5.5 shows that the setup for the Bearish 20/20 play is going to be almost identical to the setup for the Bearish Gap Surprise.

The only difference is going to be that the increase in volume is optional on this play, while it is required on the Bullish and Bearish Gap Surprises.

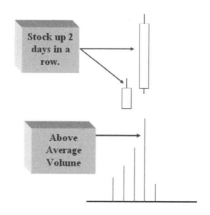

FIGURE 5.5- Bearish 20/20 Tactic Six – The Setup

The Setup / The Action

1. The stock should be up at least two days in a row.

2. We need a wide-range day of at least $1.75 point.

3. The open must be in the bottom 20% of the day's range.

4. The close must be in the top 20% of the day's range.

5. Above average volume on the current day (optional).

Stock up 2 days in a row.

Above Average Volume

For color charts go to www.traderslibrary.com/TLEcorner

The Action

Again, we are looking for the stock to not gap significantly. Stock should not gap, or should gap up or down less than 50 cents as a guideline.

When this occurs, we will be looking to short the 30-minute low. This is the abbreviated way of saying that we will let the stock trade for 30 minutes, mark off the low, and short only if it trades under that 30-minute low. That entire discussion regarding the use of the 30-minute high now applies to the 30-minute low for the Bearish 20/20 Play (Figure 5.6).

FIGURE 5.6- Bearish 20/20 Play–Tactic Six/ The Action

The Setup / **The Action**

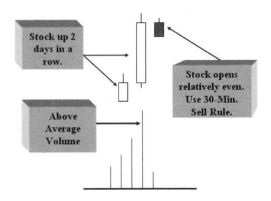

If the stock opens less then $0.50 above or below the previous day's high, wait for 30 minutes of trading to transpire. Then, sell short the stock an $0.05 – $0.10 below the low established during the first 30 minutes of trading.

Stock up 2 days in a row.

Above Average Volume

Stock opens relatively even. Use 30-Min. Sell Rule.

For color charts go to www.traderslibrary.com/TLEcorner

We set our protective stop loss for a small amount above the high of either the current day or the prior day, whichever is higher. We look for our two dollars or two-day move and exit the trade (Figure 5.7).

Figure 5.8 is a chart of Rare Hospitality Inc. (RARE), which shows an excellent example of the Bearish 20/20 Play.

The strategy on these 20/20 plays is that the stock has been moving in one direction and we have recently had a novice move in that same direction. The concept of a novice move refers to the vast majority of traders who are usually on the wrong end of most transactions and are taking positions in the stock way too late. For

FIGURE 5.7- Bearish 20/20–Tactic Six–The Action/ Place a Protective Stop

The Setup / **The Action**

Place a protective stop $0.05 to $0.10 above the current day's high or the previous day's high, *whichever is higher*.

Cover for a $2 plus profit or on the 2nd day, whichever comes first.

Stock up 2 days in a row.

Stop loss $0.05 to $0.10 above the highest high of the last two days.

Above Average Volume

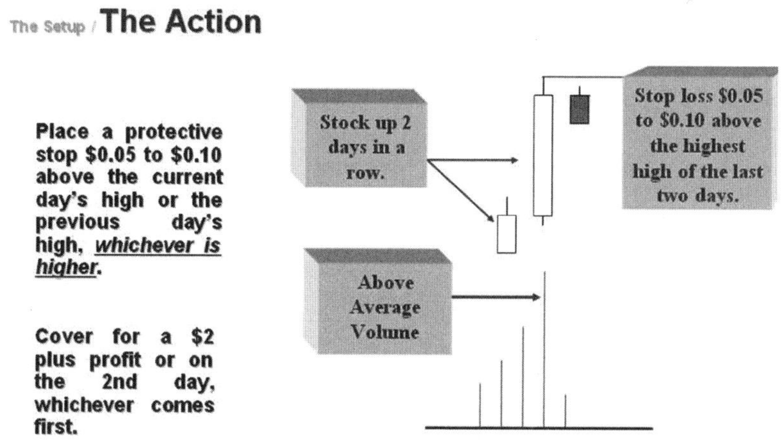

For color charts go to www.traderslibrary.com/TLEcorner

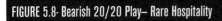

FIGURE 5.8- Bearish 20/20 Play– Rare Hospitality

RARE HOSPITALITY INC. (RARE)
Daily Chart

PSL

Two green bars, the last is a 20/20

The stock opens flat but trades under the 30-min low

For color charts go to www.traderslibrary.com/TLEcorner

example, in this chart of RARE, we have six white bars in a row, and 10 of the last 11 days are up.

The biggest white bar on the chart shows increased volume. Now here is a big question. For every buyer, there is a seller, and for every seller, there is a buyer. So who is doing the buying on that last white bar? Professionals or novices? Just as the masses are deciding the stock is worthy of being bought, the professionals are selling their shares from more than two weeks ago. The purpose of a guerrilla play is to get us on the side of the professional.

Remember that these tactics are going against the most recent trend. You need to make sure you have proof the stock will really reverse for a period of time, long enough to reach a target.

These first six guerrilla tactics have had a similar basic setup with some small differences among them. Every strategy was triggered by a different actionable event. We will now look at the remaining four tactics, which will require learning a different initial setup.

1. Bullish and Bearish 20/20 Plays are one- to two-day strategies that work best on:

   a. Low-priced stocks with limited volume.
   b. Blue Chip stocks that are usually on the "most active" list.
   c. Volatile NASDAQ stocks priced above $35 per share.
   d. Any stock that's recently had a major earnings surprise.

2. Unlike many guerrilla tactics, a Bullish 20/20 Play does not require:

   a. Two or more consecutive downward moves.
   b. A gap opening above the prior day's closing price.
   c. A wide-range day of at least $1.75 per share.
   d. Above-average volume on the day that sets up the play.

3. Bullish and Bearish 20/20 Plays are signaled when the under-lying stock does what?

   a. Opens strongly in the direction of the prevailing trend.
   b. Opens counter to the prevailing trend.
   c. Makes a generally neutral opening, then breaks above or below the high or low set in the first 30 minutes of trading.
   d. Makes a generally neutral opening and trades in a narrow range all morning.

4. A steady move upward following the opening can actually be a trap for Bullish 20//20 Play traders because:

   a. What goes up must come down.
   b. Studies have shown that stocks in a short-term uptrend actually tend to reverse at 10:00 a.m. EST.
   c. A steady up move following two downward closes attracts short sellers.
   d. If you enter after a steady up move, you may have missed most of the rally.

5. With a Bearish 20/20 Play, you want to place a protective stop where?

   a. Five to 10 cents below the previous day's low.
   b. Five to 10 cents above the previous day's high.
   c. Five to 10 cents above the current day's high.
   d. Either B or C, whichever is higher.

For answers, go to www.traderslibrary.com/TLEcorner

Chapter 6

Bear and Bull Trap Plays

For the next two plays, we are going to be using the concept of the 20/20 bar; however, there will be a few modifications. First, we are only going to require one 20/20 bar in this setup. The prior strategies required two bars, and we were reacting fairly quickly to a potential change in the stock's direction due to a gap, a 30-minute high, or low being taken out. Now we will only be reacting when the stock has already proven itself capable of making a full reversal. By some standards, the entry will be later than we normally like to take; however, the reward is usually proportionately as great.

The trap plays are also an exception because they are valid on any time frame. Remember, our first three strategies really are focused on daily charts. We're discussing gaps and 30-minute highs that did not occur on intra-day charts. The traps can happen anywhere, anytime, anyplace.

The Pristine Bear Trap

So that we stay in stride with the pattern, we will discuss the bear trap first. This is because the bear trap is the bullish pattern. It is called a bear trap because it is the bears that have been trapped. This implies bullishness and the bear trap is a long strategy.

The bear trap works accurately on all stocks and all price ranges. It is best used as a multi-day strategy and can often result in huge reversals on the daily chart. There is a catch, though, and I want you to be aware now that the stop is going to be wide on this play. We'll discuss that in a moment, but for now you should be aware that when you play a bull or bear trap, your share-sizing policies must be closely monitored.

The Setup

In simple terms, this setup requires that we have a single, very bearish day. It only needs to be one, but again, the more the better. If it is only one, we want to have a very wide bearish 20/20 bar. Although optional, if I only have one bar, I really want to see some increased volume on that bearish 20/20 bar.

Figure 6.1 shows us various examples of acceptable bear trap setups. We only need one bar, but it should be an exceptional bar. There is one other little nuance regarding the trap plays. If we have an exceptionally long 20/20 bar, we can be a lot more forgiving about the tails. The reason for this will become obvious as you look at Figure 6.2.

FIGURE 6.1- Bear Trap – Tactic Eight/ Setup

The Setup / The Action

1. **The current bar must represent a very bearish day.**
   Note: Better if has been proceeded by a multi-day down move.
2. **The open must be in the top 20% of the day's range.**
3. **The close must be in the bottom 20% of the day's range.**
4. **Above average volume on the current day (optional).**

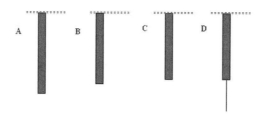

For color charts go to www.traderslibrary.com/TLEcorner

The Action

The action is going to require that we trade throughout the entire bearish bar. It does not matter if we open below the bearish 20/20 and trade straight through, or if we open approximately even and trade straight through it, or if we gap part of the way through the bearish 20/20 bar and then trade straight through. Figure 6.2 illustrates this idea.

This is the reason some tails are not that critical. In Japanese candlestick language, you may have heard of this as a "bullish engulfing bar." It is a very powerful bar. It's one of those few times in

FIGURE 6.2- Bear Trap – Tactic Eight/ Action

The Setup / **The Action**

Buy the stock $0.05 to $0.10 above the high of the prior day (the Bear day) if it's been violated. Note: Some traders may prefer to buy the stock near the close, as it is hard to determine if the stock will remain above the high of the Bear day.

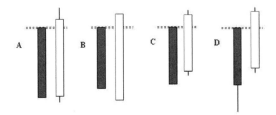

For color charts go to www.traderslibrary.com/TLEcorner

the market when the stock stands up and screams: "I can't hide it anymore! There are buyers all around me and I have to go up!"

The action is going to be to buy the stock above the high of the prior bar. The prior bar of course, is the bearish 20/20 bar.

Now for the First Word of Caution

If you are playing this on a daily chart with the intent of holding for several days, you may want to consider an alternate form of entry. It would be one that is more conservative. It requires you to wait to the end of the day and enter the stock only if the bullish reversal bar is still trading above the prior day's high. Here is the reason why: We're only interested in this play if bulls proved to be powerful enough to reverse the bearish day.

> The bear trap is only effective if it closed over the prior bar's high.

If we trade over the prior day's high and then return all the way to the low, the bulls have not proven anything. The real strength of this play comes from the bulls having the ability to close the stock above the prior day's high. Looking at it from another view, what is there to lose? With a bar as big as the current day's bar at the time it trades over the prior high, it is not likely going to get much bigger (though it could). When you consider the fact that it is a fairly frequent occurrence for the stock to sharply retrace after breaking the prior day's high, it makes sense to wait and enter the position at the end of the day only if the stock is still currently trading above the prior day's high.

The Second Word of Caution

The stop on the bear trap is going to be very wide. We need to put the stop on the other side of both of these bars. That means the stop needs to be placed under the current bar or the bearish 20/20 bar, whichever is lower (Figure 6.3). Many people shy away from the bear trap play because of the wide stop.

FIGURE 6.3- Bear Trap – Tactic Eight/ Action- Place a Protective Stop

The Setup / **The Action**

Place a protective stop $0.05 to $0.10 below the current day's low or the previous day's low, _whichever is lower_.

Cover for a $2 plus profit or on the 5th day, whichever comes first.

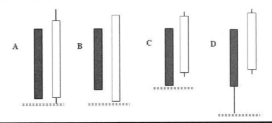

For color charts go to www.traderslibrary.com/TLEcorner

I want to point out two things that should make you consider this play, regardless of the wide stop. First, by using proper money management, you can share-size this play so that a large stop does not have to mean a large loss. It only makes sense to do if the reward-to-risk makes sense. Even though the stop is wide, the targets are often very big on a bear trap play. The target often justifies the wide stop.

Second, this is perhaps the most reliable guerrilla tactic. The fact that the stop is wide goes hand-in-hand with the reliability. However, the fact that the stock was able to reverse such a bearish move makes it unlikely that the stock will return to that low anytime soon. Anything can happen in the market, so always make sure you have an effective stop in place that makes sense for your style of trading.

The theory is this: It takes an awful lot of buying power to be able to reverse a bearish 20/20 bar in one bar. While other times we're concerned about a powerful move being extended and retracing quickly, we know this is a new move likely to continue because the bulls have the power to reverse a very bearish day (bar).

We also have a form of shock value here because we know there is a strong new commitment to the bearish side. If we have a lot of volume on the day of the bearish 20/20 bar, we know there are a lot of traders who are going to be under water at close the following day if the stock does successfully close above the prior day's high. Everyone who has committed to the short side is now in trouble.

The only remedy is to buy the stock to exit the short position. They can exit now, or they can exit later, but it is likely they will need to exit soon.

You can see an example of the bear trap in the chart of Silicon Labs Inc. in Figure 6.4. The stock was actually down for five straight days when the bulls finally engulfed the bearish 20/20 bar from the prior day. The result was five days to the upside right back to the prior breakdown.

The Bull Trap Play

Before we have any concluding comments about the trap plays,

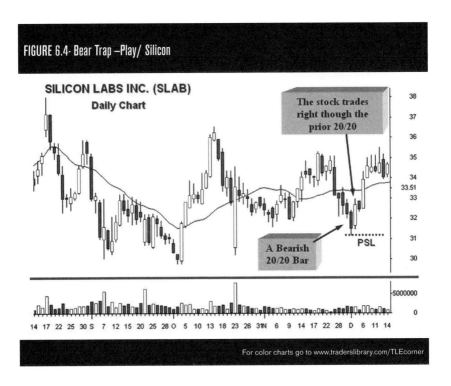

FIGURE 6.4- Bear Trap –Play/ Silicon

SILICON LABS INC. (SLAB)
Daily Chart

The stock trades right though the prior 20/20

A Bearish 20/20 Bar

PSL

For color charts go to www.traderslibrary.com/TLEcorner

let's take a look at the bull trap. Remember, the bull trap is going to be the bearish scenario because all bulls are being trapped.

The Setup

The setup and all the appropriate comments are going to be the same as we have for the bear trap. The only difference is that we need to see a very bullish day.

We want to have a bullish 20/20 bar that is long and, if possible, on increased volume, so we can be sure that we have a 100% commitment to the upside in that particular stock (Figure 6.5).

FIGURE 6.5- Bull Trap –Tactic Seven/ Setup

The Setup / The Action

1. The current bar must represent a very bullish day.
   Note: Better if has been proceeded by a multi-day upward move.
2. The open must be in the bottom 20% of the day's range.
3. The close must be in the top 20% of the day's range.
4. Above average volume on the current day (optional).

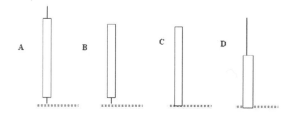

For color charts go to www.traderslibrary.com/TLEcorner

Let me talk about a few other things about the setup that can make it even more attractive. First, as I mentioned several times, if this bullish 20/20 bar is at the end of several white bars, it will be even more powerful. Second, you may find other tactics that overlap this guerrilla strategy that will make it even more effective.

For example, what if the bullish 20/20 bar came at the end of several white bars and stalled right into a prior high? What if that prior high, which is a significant major resistance area, was topped off by the flat 200-period moving average? Any of these other technical formations would help the quality of the bull trap.

The Action

Let's take a look at the action for the bull trap in Figure 6.6.

Our action will use the same concept. If the bar that forms becomes a bearish engulfing bar, we will short the stock below the low of the prior day. Remember, for all of these recent strategies, I've not been mentioning the fact that you may want to add 5 to 10 cents above or below the prior bar.

The same discussion applies to playing this strategy on the daily chart. Many traders will wait to short this until they see the stock is going to close at or below the low of the prior day. If this pattern

FIGURE 6.6- Bull Trap –Tactic Seven/ Action

The Setup / **The Action**

Short the stock $0.05 to $0.10 below the low of the prior day (the Bull day) if it's been violated. Note: Some traders may prefer to short the stock near the close, as it is hard to determine if the stock will remain below the low of the Bull day.

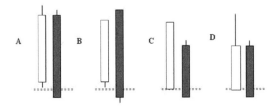

For color charts go to www.traderslibrary.com/TLEcorner

closes strong and near the high, you don't really want to be holding it as your whole strategy, since being short has now disappeared. It would force you to exit that same day at a loss.

These losses can be avoided by waiting to the end of the day. The only trade-off is it is possible the stock may fall more by the end of the day, giving you a slightly worse entry. However, considering the nature of this guerrilla play, that is a fairly small price to pay.

The same comments regarding stops and targets apply to the bull trap as I discussed with the bear trap earlier (Figure 6.7). When a bull trap occurs on exceptional volume, it can change the course

FIGURE 6.7- Bull Trap —Tactic Seven/ Action- Place a Protective Stop

The Setup / **The Action**

Place a protective stop $0.05 to $0.10 above the current day's high or the previous day's high, _whichever is higher_.

Cover for a $2 plus profit or on the 5th day, whichever comes first.

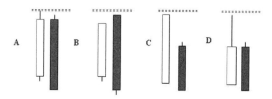

of the daily chart for weeks to come. Even though I am teaching these guerrilla tactics as one-to two-day quick hits in the market, understand that sometimes these patterns can begin a move that is worthy of a core trade (explained in Part Three).

Below in Figure 6.8 is an example of a bull trap play. The stock is Liquidity Inc. (LQDT), and the trap engulfed two bullish 20/20 bars.

Notice the volume that occurred during the bullish 20/20 bars, especially on the trap day. The chart pattern at the time the bullish 20/20 bars occurred was quite bullish and the stock appeared to be moving toward a new high. We don't know (and we do not care) what caused the stock to sell off and form the bull trap. All that

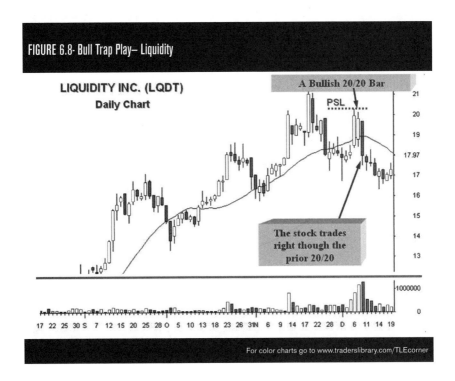

FIGURE 6.8- Bull Trap Play— Liquidity

matters is that the bull trap formed, and everyone who was long the stock from the prior two days is now in pain. This is enough to cause additional selling, which causes the stock to drop more, which causes additional selling.

Bull and bear traps are unique forms of play, even for a guerrilla tactic. They are successful a high percentage of the time, though they sometimes take a while to finish their move. That is why it is common to sometimes hold a bear or bull trap for a longer duration. While the wider stop tends to scare off some traders, the trap play remains an excellent form of guerrilla tactic and can also be used to pinpoint major reversals on daily and weekly charts.

Self-test questions

1. Bear and Bull Trap setups are recognized by looking at what kind of chart?

    a. Hourly charts.
    b. Daily charts.
    c. 10-minute charts.
    d. Charts for any time frame.

2. Bear and Bull Trap plays work on all stocks in all price ranges, but you must use what?

    a. A very narrow or tight stop.
    b. A very wide or loose stop.
    c. A flexible or trailing stop.
    d. No stop at all.

3. Unlike most other guerrilla trading plays, the Bear Trap strategy requires what?

    a. Only a single bearish 20/20 bar.
    b. Two or more consecutive bullish bars, ending with a 20/20 bar.
    c. A bearish bar followed by a bullish 20/20 bar.
    d. A very bearish bar followed by a gab opening downward.

4. The Bull Trap Play works because:

    a. A lot of buyers were drawn into the market on the strong bullish bar and will be holding losing positions they'll want to sell following the reversal.
    b. The bears demonstrated a lot of power by being able to reverse the strong bullish move in the prior period.
    c. The ability of the stock to close below the prior period's low indicates the beginning of a new move that's likely to continue.
    d. All of the above.

5. For a Bull Trap Play to ultimately be successful, the initial bearish bar must be the result of what?

    a. A negative report that weakens the stock's fundamentals.
    b. A downgrade by one or more leading market analysts.
    c. A breakdown through a technical support level.
    d. It's not necessary to know – nor do we care – what caused the initial bearish move.

For answers, go to www.traderslibrary.com/TLEcorner

Chapter 7

The Pristine Bullish and Bearish Mortgage Play

It is time for the final two tactics, and in this case I may have saved the best for last. We are going to discuss the Bullish and Bearish Mortgage Plays. The mortgage play is really a variation on the trap play and, in a sense, may be thought of as a combination of the trap play and the gap surprise play. This is because the mortgage play accomplishes the job that the trap does, but does it with more shock value than any gap surprise play could ever deliver.

Similar to the trap play, the mortgage play can be highly successful, but also can deliver substantial losses if not played properly. The stop on the mortgage play is going to be as wide as the stop on the trap plays, so the same cautions must be used.

Bullish Mortgage Play

Let's look first at the Bullish Mortgage Play. It works best as a 3- to 10-day trading tactic, and on volatile NASDAQ stocks above $35 per share. But if it sets up properly, this play should be used on NASDAQ or listed at any price range.

The Setup

The setup is the same as what is required for a trap play. In simple terms, this setup requires that we have a single very bearish day (Figure 7.1). It only needs to be one, but again, the more the bet-

FIGURE 7.1- Bullish Mortgage Play – Tactic Nine/ Setup

The Setup / The Action

Bar 1 must be a bearish 20/20 bar. This is the bar that indicates that a large number of traders have sold. Note: The smaller the upper and lower tails on Bar 1 the better.

The Mortgage Play is only a two-bar strategy.

A   B

For color charts go to www.traderslibrary.com/TLEcorner

ter. If it is only one, I want to have a very wide bearish 20/20 bar. While it is optional, if I only have one bar, I really want to see some increased volume on that bearish 20/20 bar.

We have seen this setup. It is simple and the same as the trap plays. However, that is where the similarity ends.

The Action

The action is simple as well—simple but extremely powerful. We will take action as a Bullish Mortgage Play if the stock is able to gap over the entire black bar. This means the opening trade of the

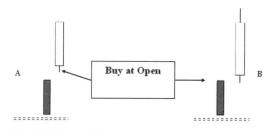

FIGURE 7.2- Bullish Mortgage Play – Tactic Nine/ Action

The Setup / **The Action**

Immediately buy at the market when Bar 2 opens above the high of Bar 1. Note: This signifies that now every hedge fund, trader, and investor who sold short during Bar 1 is now in negative territory. All shorts are thrown for a loop.

A   Buy at Open   B

day must be above the high of the prior bar, the bearish 20/20 bar. Take a look at Figure 7.2.

Please note: The gap that has occurred is not simply from the top of the first bar to the bottom of the second bar. Remember, the stock closed the first day at the bottom of the black bar. This means the gap was huge. This action is similar to the bear trap because it has made every bear from the prior day a loser. We are going to enter this play immediately at the open. Again, you may remember my discussion earlier that you may opt to wait a few seconds to make sure the stock is heading in the desired direction. These plays can be quite volatile when they open.

FIGURE 7.3- Bullish Mortgage Play– Tactic Nine/ Place Your Stop

The Setup / **The Action**

Place your stop just below the low of Bar 1. Note: _This makes this tactic very high risk_.

Use a trailing stop strategy until a) your objective has been met, b) the low of a reversal bar has been violated or c) a gap up occurs. Or simply ride the trade for 10 days.

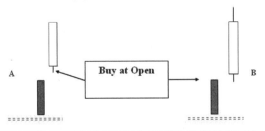

For color charts go to www.traderslibrary.com/TLEcorner

The reason these are a buy at the open and that we are not that concerned about the volatility is because of our protective stop loss.

The stop is going to be on the other side of the bearish 20/20 bar (Figure 7.3). This means it can absorb a lot of volatility without coming near the stop. The average mortgage play should last about 10 days. This, of course, is a very general guideline. What you'll usually see happen is that the stock will make a quick run to the upside for at least a couple of days, and then pull back before running the second time. At that point, the power of the mortgage play has pretty much played itself out, and it is time to exit.

Example of a Bullish Mortgage Play

Let's take a look at an example of a Bullish Mortgage Play shown in Figure 7.4. I want to run through this play as it happens so you understand the emotional state of the average trader, as well as why some of these guerrilla tactics give us an edge in the market.

Let's pick up on the chart on the day before the bearish 20/20 bar. The stock was then going sideways, with little activity or volume. Then, on the day before the bearish 20/20 bar, the stock put in a fair-sized black bar that traded below the lows of the last two week's worth of trading on increased volume. This was a heads up to everybody to be watching the stock for a short on the following day. Everyone was watching the following day, and as stock continued to trade lower, you can see why people were exiting their long positions while shorts were piling in. The stock traded below

FIGURE 7.4- Bullish Mortgage Play/ Dress Barn

DRESS BARN INC. (DBRN)
Daily Chart

The stock GAPS over the prior 20/20

A Bearish 20/20 Bar

PSL

For color charts go to www.traderslibrary.com/TLEcorner

the low of the last month on huge volume and closed at the low of the day.

Sometimes I point out the errors of new traders and how, at times, these are opportunities for others to capitalize. In this case, however, even the most experienced trader could have been holding this stock short at the close. Usually this pattern will follow through to the downside, as it is a very bearish breakdown.

> Many of these guerrilla plays have "shock value" that can have traders buying and selling out of pure necessity, often having nothing to do with the reason why the stock gapped initially.

So, the next morning, everyone will wake up to a small problem. Even the best entry from the prior day would have you short somewhere around $21.50. Those shorting later in the day would have an entry around $21.50, and there are a lot of traders somewhere in between those two numbers. They all have one thing in common. No matter who they are or when they shorted, they will all be losing money when the market opens the following day. Some could be down very large amounts of money.

When I say large, I don't mean it as an absolute term. I mean it as a relative term. In other words, one trader may be down $5,000, but that amount of money is meaningless to him or her. Another trader could be down $5,000, and it could be most of his or her account. What matters is the relative pain that individual traders are feeling. Anybody who risked a full amount of money with a tight stop is going to be in a lot of pain the following morning because of a large gap.

What's the only answer to solve the problem? The traders must exit their positions. And, in order to exit a short position, you must buy the stock. This purchase is no different than buying the stock to be long.

By the way, as the stock begins to trade above the base for the first time, there are a lot of traders to want to be long. So we have longs piling in to a bullish position, we have shorts who need to cover their underwater positions, and you can see how the snowball effect develops. If you were in a lot of pain that morning from being short but decided to wait, your pain increased at an exponential rate every five minutes. Eventually you have to push the exit button. That, of course, drives the stock higher and causes more traders to push the exit button.

Now, you may be asking a very common question. Why did the stock gap up this morning? The answer to this question is one that, if you understand, you'll never again look at fundamentals or news the same way. The answer: We simply do not care what made the stock gap up. There probably was a reason. They may have done earnings that day, or the company may simply have had a positive announcement to make. They may have unveiled a new product, or an analyst may have upgraded them. The company may have come out and negated a rumor that made the stock fall the prior day.

As a matter of fact, perhaps the news announcement that made the stock gap up was bad news. This happens more than you would think.

Here is why we don't care: Let's say you shorted the stock in the afternoon of the breakdown on the bearish 20/20 day. Let's say you shorted at $20.75 with a protective stop loss at $21 based on an intraday pattern. Let's say you were risking $1,000. The stock closed in your favor about the same distance as it was to your stop. Therefore, you would be in the money about $1,000. Many traders may actually add to their position at that point, hoping for the gap down the next day. But let's just say you hung on to your existing shares. When the stock opened the next day, it gapped five times past your stop. This meant you were down $5,000 at the open.

> Remember, it is the emotions of greed and fear that move stocks. It is most evident on some of these guerrilla plays.

You freeze like a deer in headlights, but every time you glance at your position minder, you see it is falling like a rock. As a matter of fact, it is dropping an additional $1,000 every time the stock rallies 25 cents. Guess what? The stock rallied 25 cents more 10 times throughout this day. That is a lot of pain to be sitting through.

Now the $64,000 question. While you are sitting through all of this, does it matter to you whether the stock gapped because of a good earnings report or because of an analyst downgrade? Do you hang on to your position if the news announcement was "bad" news because you assume the stock must eventually drop? These gaps that shock can hit pain buttons inside of traders that force the purchase or sale of stock regardless of the reason for the price movements, even if you are a fundamental-type trader.

The Bearish Mortgage Play

And now for our final tactic—the Bearish Mortgage Play. I will run through the setup and action very quickly because you should have the hang of this by now.

The Bearish Mortgage Play works best as a 3- to 10- day trading tactic. It works best on volatile NASDAQ stocks above $35 per share, but if it sets up properly, this play should be played on NASDAQ or listed at any price range.

FIGURE 7.5· Bearish Mortgage Play– Tactic Ten/ Setup

The Setup / The Action

Bar 1 must be a bullish 20/20 bar. This is the bar that indicates that a large number of longs have been committed. Note: The smaller the upper and lower tails on Bar 1 the better.

The Mortgage Play is only a two-bar strategy.

For color charts go to www.traderslibrary.com/TLEcorner

The Setup

The setup is the same as the Bullish Mortgage Play, except in reverse. We need a single very bullish day. It only needs to be one, but again, the more the better. If it is only one, you want to have a very wide bullish 20/20 bar. While it is optional, if I only have one bar, I really want to see some increased volume on that bullish 20/20 bar.

Figure 7.5 shows the one bar setup necessary for the Bearish Mortgage Play.

The Action

The same simple but very powerful action is what we want to see for this play. Here we need the stock to gap under the bullish wide range bar. We will take action as a Bearish Mortgage Play if the stock is able to gap under the entire white bar. This means the opening trade of the day must be under the low of the prior bar, the bullish 20/20 bar. Take a look at Figure 7.6.

Again, notice the nature and severity of this gap. The gap that has occurred is not simply from the bottom of the first bar to the top of the second bar. Remember, the stock closed the first day at the top

FIGURE 7.6- Bearish Mortgage Play– Tactic Ten/ Action

The Setup / **The Action**

Immediately short at the market when Bar 2 opens below the low of Bar 1. Note: This signifies that now every hedge fund, mutual fund, trader, and investor who bought during Bar 1 is now in negative territory. All longs are thrown for a loop.

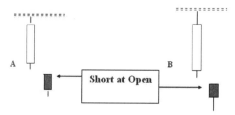

of the white bar. This means the gap was huge. This action is similar to the bull trap because it has made every bull from the prior day a loser. We are going to enter this play immediately at the open. You may remember my discussion earlier that you may opt to wait a few seconds to make sure the stock is heading in the desired direction. These plays can be quite volatile when they open.

The reason that we are going to short this stock at the open, and that we are not very concerned about the volatility, is because of our protective stop loss (Figure 7.7).

The stop is going to be on the other side of the bullish 20/20 bar. This means it can absorb a lot of volatility without coming near the

FIGURE 7.7- Bearish Mortgage Play– Tactic Ten/ Action- Place Your Stop

The Setup / **The Action**

Place your stop just over the high of Bar 1. Note: *This makes this tactic very high risk.*

Use a trailing stop strategy until a) your objective has been met, b) the high of a reversal bar has been violated or c) a gap down occurs. <u>Or simply hold the trade for 10 days.</u>

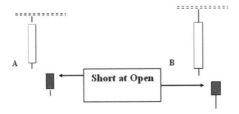

For color charts go to www.traderslibrary.com/TLEcorner

stop. The average mortgage play should last about 10 days. This is a very general guideline. What you'll usually see happen is that the stock will make a quick run to the upside for at least a couple of days and then pull back before running the second time. At that point, the power of the mortgage play has pretty much played itself out, and it is time to exit.

An Example

As I ran through the example of the Bullish Mortgage Play, you may have had a few lightbulbs go off in terms of why technical analysis works in different situations. Perhaps it helped you to see how the emotional states dominate the market and why stocks rarely fall purely because of supply and demand issues. Those supply and demand issues are driven by people's emotional states.

Take a look at Figure 7.8, and I will run through the rationale of this chart pattern.

The stock here is HSIC and it has been going sideways on this daily chart for quite a while. You can see how, in the beginning of November, it appeared to make a move down, but that move failed. This is a bullish sign when you see a failed breakdown such as this. At the beginning of December, the stock put in a couple medium-size white bars. The second bar appears to be breaking across the top of that long consolidation.

The next morning apparently everyone liked this new breakout and a big white bar develops. It is the biggest one on the chart and eas-

FIGURE 7.8- Bearish Mortgage Play/ Schein Henry

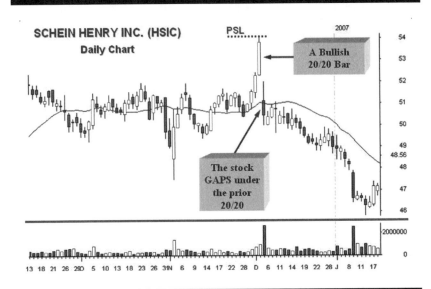

SCHEIN HENRY INC. (HSIC)
Daily Chart

A Bullish 20/20 Bar

The stock GAPS under the prior 20/20

For color charts go to www.traderslibrary.com/TLEcorner

ily qualifies for our bullish 20/20 bar. It closed near the high of the day and all of the bulls were quite happy. This includes the bulls who played the stock early on the first white bar, or the bulls who played the immediate breakout on the second white bar, and even all bulls who bought the bullish 20/20 bar. Even those who bought at the end of the bullish 20/20 bar were not feeling any pain as the stock closed near the high of the day.

Then, the next morning the wake-up call came. The stock opened under the low of the bullish 20/20 bar and of the prior white bar. Every single person who entered a long position in the prior two days, was, at that time, in a lot of pain. What is the only remedy to fix this pain? They needed to sell their position, and most of them needed to sell it pretty quickly.

The stock had a pretty volatile first day of trading after the gap, as you can see by the long tails. However, notice the longer-term effect of this Bearish Mortgage Play. The stock dropped almost nonstop for six continuous weeks.

Novice Moves

Now here is a bonus lesson for you to conclude this chapter. After the Bearish Mortgage Play, and after the stock dropped for six straight weeks, what do you see at the end of that drop? We find a bearish 20/20 bar. It came at the end of the move. This is what we call a novice move down or a novice 20/20 bar. After dropping for six weeks, these people were just then getting out of their position.

Do you think those were professional traders selling at this level or novices reacting to their emotional state? Selling was the right thing to do, but it should have taken place a long time ago. Also, take a look at the volume that is associated with this bearish wide range bar. This bar will usually end the move down; the move that was created from the Bearish Mortgage Play.

The mortgage plays are very powerful movers of stock. They're great for 3- to 10-day holds. They are also wonderful for setting long-term tops and bottoms in individual stocks, and even in the market as a whole. If you don't believe me, just take a look at your charts. Print out the market, or some of your favorite charts, and go through and circle the major highs and lows, and the reversal points, which have been formed over the weeks. You may not have realized it before, but you have just learned some of the reasons why these reversals happen. The vast majority of them are either from a guerrilla tactic, or a climactic buy or climactic sell setup.

Self-test questions

1. The Pristine Mortgage Play is what?

   a. A variation of the Bearish 20/20 Bar Play.
   b. A combination of the Trap Play and the Gap Surprise Play.
   c. A strategy that works best with shares of real estate investment trusts.
   d. An entirely new type of bullish technical strategy.

2. When looking at a setup for a Bullish Mortgage Play, you want to see:

   a. A single bearish bar with a small body and long shadows.
   b. Two or more consecutive bullish bars of any size.
   c. A single bearish 20/20 bar with a wide body and very small upper and lower tails.
   d. A bearish 20/20 bar followed by a 20/20 bullish bar.

3. Entry to a Bullish or Bearish Mortgage Play should be made when?

   a. As soon as possible at the opening on the following day.
   b. On a minor reversal 30 minutes after the next day's opening.
   c. Five minutes after the opening, but only if the price is above or below the prior day's high or low.
   d. Near the close the following day if the price is above or below the prior day's high or low.

4. The stop for a Bullish Mortgage Play should be placed where?

   a. Five or 10 cents below the price at which you bought the stock.
   b. Twenty-five cents below the current day's low price.
   c. Just above the prior day's closing price.
   d. Just below the low of the prior day's candlestick bar.

5. While they have a very reliable record, because of the placement of the stop, Mortgage Plays tend to be what?

   a. Fairly low-risk strategies.
   b. Very high-risk strategies.
   c. Subject to a fairly early forced exit.
   d. Suitable for "set it and forget it" traders.

For answers, go to www.traderslibrary.com/TLEcorner

Chapter 8
Putting It All Together

In conclusion of my discussion on guerrilla trading, I would like to touch on a few subjects. First, I have mentioned several times that these guerrilla tactics can at times change the direction of the daily chart. I would like to show you some examples of this. Second, I want to give you some instruction on how to find these plays. Third, I want to give you some additional instructions on picking targets for the guerrilla plays.

Guerrillas Reverse Charts

Figure 8.1 is the daily chart of Microchip Technologies (MCHP).

When you look back at daily charts of stocks or indexes, they will always have certain things in common. Most stocks will spend the

FIGURE 8.1- Guerrilla Plays Reversing Charts

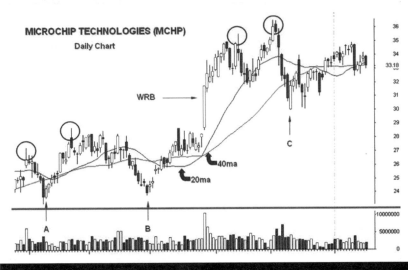

MICROCHIP TECHNOLOGIES (MCHP)
Daily Chart

WRB

40ma
20ma

C

A   B

For color charts go to www.traderslibrary.com/TLEcorner

majority of their time trading in a sloppy, non-directional pattern. You will always find some trends, and you will always find key areas on the chart that set significant highs or lows that last weeks or months.

When stocks are in a nice trend, a consistent pattern develops. These are the ones that we like to trade most of the time. They have a clean uptrend, a clean downtrend, or even a clean sideways trend. What happens when the stock breaks tradition and decides to change trend? Or if it falls abruptly then reverses? It is usually a guerrilla tactic that sets tops and bottoms, and does so with amazing accuracy.

> Guerrilla tactics can be used to help find long term tops and bottoms on daily and weekly charts.

Let's talk about Figure 8.1. MCHP is, generally speaking, in an uptrend, as shown by higher highs and higher lows. Since we are in an uptrend, I simply identified the long-term bottoms that were formed. These are arrows A, B, and C. Were any of these areas playable? Let's take a look.

Arrow A is a Bullish 20-20 Play. We have several days down, and then that last big black bar just before the arrow. The stock had six lower highs, and then had the largest selloff (black) bar in recent history. This is a nice bearish 20/20 bar that sets up the play. This happens on increased volume. The stock opened flat the next day, and the strategy is to go long over the high of the day after 30 minutes of trading. This set a low that was not violated any time in the near future. Besides being a viable trade, this was a high volume guerrilla tactic that changed the short-term direction of the daily chart.

Let's look at arrow B. You should know this now as a minor Bullish Mortgage Play. I use the word minor because the bar is not above-average in length. The pullback going into B is starting to look bearish. We were not able to stay above the moving averages, and the pullback challenges the prior low. Going into B, we have four lower highs (six out of seven also). Then the 20/20 bar forms. The next day, the stock gaps open just above the high of the prior day's bar. Note that MCHP closed at the bottom of that black bar, then opened the next day near the top. The stock sets a higher low, which is not violated any time in the near future. Again a guerrilla tactic has changed the direction of the chart.

Next we have arrow C. This, of course, is the guerrilla tactic known as a Gap and Snap Play. Again, five days down followed by a bearish 20/20 bar. This time, the stock gaps down, setting up the long entry as the stock penetrates the low of the prior day. Again, MCHP sets a higher low, which is not violated any time in the near future. Look at the increased volume at the low. Once again, it is a high volume guerrilla tactic that changed the short-term direction of the daily chart.

While all these bottoms made for nice profits as a one- to two-day trading tactic, they also set lows on the chart that could have been traded on a swing or core basis.

Don't just take my word for it. Print out the daily charts of your favorite stocks and circle all of the significant highs and lows that have been set over the year. See how many you can now identify as a guerrilla tactic. Prior to reading this book, it is likely you had very little knowledge of why a stock might have reversed where it did. Now, when you look, you will discover that one-third to one-half of the reversals on the daily chart will be a result of a guerrilla tactic that you learned in this book.

How to Find Guerrilla Tactics

Scanning for guerrilla tactics is fairly simple but can also be quite tedious if you're not very organized. Let's discuss a couple of different ways to get prepared for guerrilla tactics every morning, and then look at a couple of ways to find the guerrilla tactics throughout the day.

As I discuss ways to do this, I am going go to be mentioning the option you may want to rely on: a computerized scan that will automatically pick out your setups. To find something like a bullish 20/20 bar, you would have to become very familiar with a scanning package to enter the parameters needed to find a bar. I use Pristine ESP™, which eliminates the need to program anything yourself. Pristine ESP is incredible scanning software that already has all the parameters built in for all of the Pristine setups.

There are dozens and dozens of tactics built in that go well beyond the setups you are learning in this book. If using Pristine ESP, you simply go to the guerrilla trading scans and pull up one of the different lists for various Pristine guerrilla tactics. A list of stocks that have met the requirements I have described in this book will pop into your charting package.

Computerized scans such as Pristine ESP™ can help shorten your preparation time.

Getting Organized

Preparing for the day is a fairly easy task. If you noticed, all of the guerrilla tactics have one thing in common. They all revolve around a 20/20 bar. So our first job when scanning is to go through your entire universe and simply look for bullish or bearish 20/20 bars.

You notice I mention going through your "universe." There are thousands of stocks in the market, and you simply do not have time to go through that many stocks one by one. Many of these are penny-stocks, or trade with such light volume that you would never trade them. So your job in creating your own personal universe is to develop a list of stocks you feel comfortable scanning every night. You may create yours by combining several lists of stocks that you like, such as the Dow 30, the NASDAQ 100, and the semiconductor stocks.

Another way to create your list would be to filter out everything you don't want to see, such as stocks that are priced under a certain dollar amount, or stocks that trade under a certain volume. These numbers will be different for every trader because everyone has different account sizes and different share sizes they are willing to purchase to hold overnight. Another method of creating your own personal universe is to simply use one of the built-in universes that can be found in the Pristine ESP.

> A trader's universe of stocks is a subset of all tradable stocks that includes the biggest total list of stocks a trader would ever use for trading.

So, you can prepare for the day by either going through your personal universe manually or by using the lists prepared each night by Pristine ESP. If you are using the list given to you by Pristine ESP, you still must go through it to make sure the setups meet your standards. Pristine ESP will err on the side of including every possible play so that you, the user, may discard what you feel to be low quality.

Once you have your list completed and the market is ready to open, things are a little different when you are guerrilla trading as opposed to some other forms of trading.

For example, you will not be able to set any alarms or place any buy-stop or sell-stop orders before the market opens. When you are swing trading and day trading, you may have pre-assigned areas on the chart that will become your entry points. These points may not change and can be used as entries anytime after the market opens. This is not true with guerrilla trades. Just because we have identified a 20/20 bar, we do not know the possible entries until the market opens the next day. Remember, we will have different entries if the stock gaps up, gaps down, or doesn't happen all.

So, the first thing we're going to do in the morning is check our watch list, which is full of bullish and bearish 20/20 bars, to see if any of the stocks are gapping. Any stock that is showing a gap should be evaluated to see if it meets requirements for either a Gap Surprise Play, or a Gap and Snap/Gap and Crap Play. A large gap may qualify for a Bullish or Bearish Mortgage Play.

If the stock is not gapping, we have to look at the 30-minute high or low for a Bullish or Bearish 20/20 Play, and if there is only a one-bar setup, we have to wait for the entire bar to be engulfed to qualify as the trap play. Notice all these different strategies have different entries and none of them can be determined until the trading day begins.

> Staying organized in the morning is required when guerrilla trading because many of the plays find entries early in the day, even in the first few minutes.

The key is to stay very organized in the morning. Immediately begin qualifying plays that may have quicker entries so they can be watched for an entry if they do qualify. Get familiar with using the alarm program on your charting package to set alarms for the plays that may come later in the day.

The Reward to Risk Ratio

These guerrilla tactics I have shown you have something else in common as well. Their focus is really on the setup and the entry. Usually in trading, we clearly identify a firm target so that we may develop a reward-to-risk scenario by comparing the target to the stop. The reward-to-risk is the amount to be made from the entry to the target, as compared to the amount to be lost from the entry to the stop. While this still must be a consideration when guerrilla trading, there are some unique things about guerrilla trading that make this less of an emphasis.

First, the reward-to-risk relationship does not exist in a vacuum. It is closely tied to the probabilities of success. In other words, you may have a certain reward-to-risk relationship you require to take a trade. However, wouldn't you be just as interested in the trade even if the reward-to-risk relationship was much lower or if the trade were successful a huge majority of the time? This is the first unique thing about guerrilla trading. While some of the reward-to-risk ratios are lower, properly set up guerrilla tactics are highly successful.

> The reward-to-risk ratio is the projected target amount divided by the projected stop amount. Many traders will require a certain number in order to take the trade.

The second issue with targets on guerrilla trades is that this is the only time we're not working in a pre-defined area on the chart. In other words, when we're swing trading, we know exactly where the entry is going to be if it occurs at all, and we know the general area that we expect to reach based on the chart before us. This is not the way it works with guerrilla tactics. They often involve gaps that can take us far away from the current area on the chart.

Also, being a one- to two-day trading tactic, we offer one target idea of holding two days. This is because after one to two days, it is not easy to find a target area on the daily chart. While this is a general guideline, you may want to develop more exact targets as you get good at these plays. It is possible you may hit the best price on day one, and find a retracement on day two.

Some traders may also look to sell incrementally. They may sell some on day one, and hold some shares for day two. Looking on intraday charts to find significant support or resistance levels is a way to help find areas to sell some shares. Figures 8.2 and 8.3 are examples.

The first of these, Figure 8.2, is a daily chart of Intercontinental Exchange Inc. The chart shows a Gap and Crap Play that made the stock fall for four straight days. However, at the end of day two and the beginning of day three, the stock was at its smallest profit level of the entire fall. The majority of profits could be found near the end of day one or at the end of day three. Here is an example where a two-day hold did not yield the best results, even though the play was an excellent one.

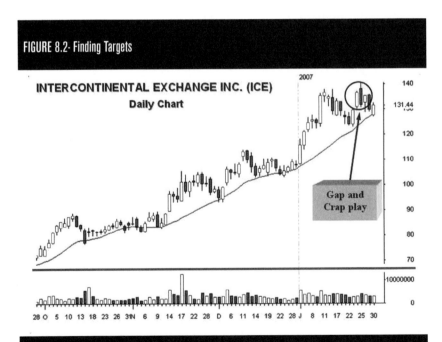

FIGURE 8.2- Finding Targets

Let's take a look at how the target could have been refined better. Take a look at Figure 8.3. This is the 15-minute chart that covers the first day and a half the stock fell from the guerrilla play. By looking to the left, we can see support and resistance files that might impede the stock during its drop. The concept of using intraday charts and finding support and resistance levels to help determine where a stock may turn is a whole other topic in trading and technical analysis. However, I want to show you an example of how some of these skills can be used to help refine even the guerrilla plays.

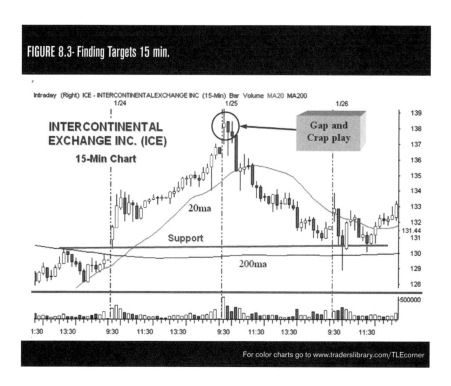

FIGURE 8.3- Finding Targets 15 min.

You can see that on the morning of the 24th, the stock gapped up slightly. Notice the area between where the stock opened that day, where it closed the prior day, and the prior high on the 23rd that the support line is sitting on. This whole general area will serve as support for several reasons. One of them is the concept of support that is found when a gap is filled.

Perhaps you've heard of this before. During the day on the 25th, the stock dropped in a very nice, even manner. There were no extreme sell-offs and no strong counter-rallies. When a stock falls that cleanly for that extended period of time, it will usually respond to its first area of support. This would be an excellent area to cover some of the shares from this Gap and Crap Play.

It is only at the end of the first day, but many traders may want to lighten up on the overnight position if they had a large share size from the start of the play. Also, the stock had a significant drop and we know a retracement will be likely. It may take more than two days for the stock to return to prior lows, which would take it beyond the normal holding time that we want to be in a guerrilla play.

You can see that setting multiple targets and involving intraday charts will open the door to incremental selling and using guerrilla trades as the entries to day trades. If used properly, this can help expand the use of this strategy.

Summary

For many people who are part-time traders, the guerrilla tactics can be an excellent method of trading a shorter time frame than swing and core trades. If the trader is able to be with the market for the first hour of the day, many of these positions can be entered during that time. Then, through the use of computer-aided buy-stops and sell-stops, the position can be effectively managed while away at work.

For the full-time trader, the guerrilla tactics offer an excellent complement to many other strategies because they often thrive in choppy sideways market environments.

I have shared with you some of the most treasured tactics that our Pristine-trained traders use. The guerrilla tactics make for a unique style of trading that can be used in any market environment. These tactics are nothing more than us capitalizing on short term transitions from fear to greed. We are waiting for several days of pain in order to step up to be buyers, simply because no one can stand the pain anymore. And then, we're waiting for several days of greed. We're waiting for the confidence level to be so high and then for that moment when everyone is already committed, to squeeze them in a short scenario.

Self-test questions

1. A study of charts looking for guerrilla trading opportunities will show what?

    a. Stocks tend to trend higher most of the time.

    b. Stocks tend to trend lower most of the time.

    c. Stocks tend to spend the majority of their time trading in a sloppy, non-directional pattern.

    d. Stocks tend to trade flat most of the time, moving in a very narrow range.

2. Guerrilla trading tactics can be used to find what on daily and weekly charts?

    a. Rising or falling trend lines.

    b. Long-term tops or bottoms for the stock being tracked.

    c. Key moving average lines for different time periods.

    d. Reaction points that follow key fundamental news releases.

3. The key to finding opportunities to use guerrilla trading tactics is to get organized, which includes:

    a. Narrowing the "universe" of stocks you'll be monitoring.

    b. Finding a computerized scanning package, such as Pristine ESP, to help you monitor the market.

    c. Devising a set of filters to eliminate situations you don't want to see.

    d. All of the above.

4. A 20/20 bar by itself doesn't necessarily signal a guerrilla trading opportunity. You also need to see:

   a. What happened in the periods before the 20/20 bar.
   b. How the stock closes in the period following the 20/20 bar.
   c. How the stock behaves at the opening in the period following the 20/20 bar.
   d. Whether the overall market is moving in the same direction.

5. An important element in selecting a guerrilla trading tactic is the reward-to-risk ratio, which you determine by:

   a. Subtracting the stock's closing price from its opening price on bearish trades.
   b. Subtracting the stop-loss amount from the desired target amount.
   c. Dividing the projected target amount by the projected stop-loss amount.
   d. Subtracting the stock's current price from the projected target amount.

For answers, go to www.traderslibrary.com/TLEcorner

PART 2

Micro Trading

Chapter 9

Charting Tools of the Microtrader

Now, let's talk about the trading style known as microtrading. It covers a holding period anywhere from seconds to hours. It does not call for holding stocks overnight. This style of active trading goes after small, but frequent bite-size gains. The microtrader typically uses two time frames. Not a weekly time frame, not a daily, but two dominant intraday time frames—the 5-minute and the 15-minute.

Figures 9.1 and 9.2 are examples of two microtrading charts. They are the 15-minute time frame and the 5-minute time frame (respectively), and they are from the same stock at the same time. Remember, on a 5-minute chart, every bar represents 5 minutes worth of trading, and on a 15-minute chart, every bar represents 15 minutes worth of trading. Remember also that we are looking

Intraday (Right) NVLS - NOVELLUS SYS INC (15-Min) Bar Volume MA20 MA200

15-Minute Chart

20ma

200ma

Color coded volume bars...

For color charts go to www.traderslibrary.com/TLEcorner

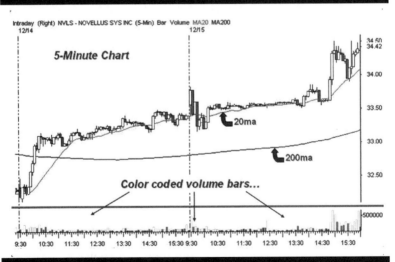

Intraday (Right) NVLS - NOVELLUS SYS INC (5-Min) Bar Volume MA20 MA200

5-Minute Chart

20ma

200ma

Color coded volume bars...

For color charts go to www.traderslibrary.com/TLEcorner

at the same price pattern being viewed, first through the eyes of the 15- minute chart, then through the eyes of the 5-minute chart. The 5-minute offers us a closer look. It is a zoomed-in or magnified look at the same price pattern.

The staple for a microtrader is the 5-minute time frame. The 15-minute becomes important during certain parts of the day, and we'll talk about that a little later. But, the window through which the microtrader views virtually every single thing that goes on in the market will be the 5-minute time frame.

Figure 9.2 is a 5-minute chart with two moving averages. Every single intraday time frame shown, such as the 5-minute time frame and the 15-minute time frame, will have two dominant moving averages displayed at all times. They are the 20-period simple moving average and the 200-period moving average. In fact, the 200-period moving average is incredibly powerful in the intraday time frame.

Stocks obey the 200-period moving average in amazing fashion. If it's rallying up to the 200-period moving average, you can bet your bottom dollar, 8 or 9 times out of every 10, that the 200-period moving average will stop it dead in its tracks. If the stock is coming down to its 200-period moving average, you can bet your bottom dollar again that the 200-period moving average will stop the decline dead in its tracks. We have a variety of microtrading tactics built around this frequent occurrence.

The Power of the Moving Averages

Let's take a look at how the 20- and 200-period moving averages are used by the microtrader. It is amazing how often and how accurately prices respond to these moving averages. If you look at Figure 9.3, you will see an example of an occurrence you can find happening throughout every trading day on a multitude of stocks.

This is a 5-minute chart of the stock of Apple Computer Inc. You are viewing just over one day's worth of trading. On this particular day, the stock gapped down. This means it opened at a price that was significantly below the closing price of the previous day. You can see the void on the left side of the chart where the stock

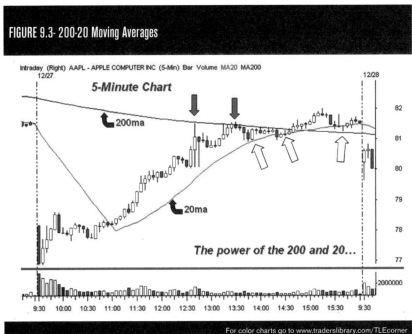

FIGURE 9.3- 200-20 Moving Averages

gapped down in between these two prices. On this particular day, Apple became very bullish and rallied hard. Then, at 12:45 p.m., the strongest part of the rally came, but the stock died as it ran into the 200-period moving average. You can see that topping tail left behind on what was the biggest white bar of the rally.

This event happens very frequently. As a matter of fact, it is a rule of thumb in itself that any rally or decline will likely reverse when coming in contact with a flat 200-period moving average.

Now, remember, they are not going to stop or halt a stock 100% of the time. That is fine because that is not what we are looking for. As a trader, you are a probability specialist, which means that you play the odds. We look for something that happens a lot more times than it doesn't happen, and we capitalize on those odds by doing it over and over again.

> Sharp rallies and declines are often halted by a flat or nearly flat 200-period moving average.

Now notice what happens. The stock pulls back over a 30-minute period or so, then attempts to break through the 200-period moving average for a second time. Again it is foiled. Think of the price as being similar to a wrecking ball coming into the wall formed by the 200-period moving average. Every time the wrecking ball attacks the wall, it weakens it a bit.

Note what happens on the next pullback. Price encounters the rising 20-period moving average. The stock is supported (at the first white arrow) and is propelled all the way back into the flat 200-period moving average. Just like that wrecking ball, this weakens the 200-period moving average a little more. Again, the stock tries to decline but is caught by the rising 20-period moving average at the second white arrow.

> Rising moving averages often serve as support. Declining moving averages often serve as resistance.

This time, the stock finally breaks through and continues higher. Notice at the third arrow that, after breaking through, the first pullback now finds support on the flat 200-period moving average. Rising moving averages often serve as support. Declining moving averages often serve as resistance. Remember, at the moment, I am not even showing you any tactics. We will get to those shortly. These are simply occurrences that happen in the market a high percentage of the time.

Self-test questions

1. Microtrading is a style of trading in which positions are held for how long?

    a. From seconds to hours.
    b. From hours to days.
    c. From days to weeks.
    d. From weeks to months.

2. Microtraders clarify the outlook for a potential strategy by what?

    a. Expanding out to a chart covering longer trading periods.
    b. Zooming in to a chart with shorter trading periods.
    c. Watching the same chart for two more trading periods.
    d. Drawing a trendline to better define the stock's directional tendency.

3. Of all the intraday moving averages, stocks tend to obey which one most faithfully?

    a. The 10-period simple moving average.
    b. The 20-period exponential moving average.
    c. The 100-period logarithmic moving average.
    d. The 200-period simple moving average.

4. As a general rule of thumb, which of the following is true?

    a. A stock in a rally will likely turn lower when it runs up against a flat 200-day moving average.

    b. A stock in a decline will likely turn higher when it drops into contact with a flat 200-day moving average.

    c. Both of the above.

    d. None of the above.

5. In microtrading, a moving average line that is rising often serves as what?

    a. A level of resistance.

    b. A point of convergence.

    c. A level of support.

    d. The precursor of a potential tend reversal.

For answers, go to www.traderslibrary.com/TLEcorner

Chapter 10

Timing Tools of the Microtrader

Market timing tools include the NASDAQ Future's Contract, the S&P Future's Contract, the New York Stock Exchange TICK indicator, the NASDAQ TICK indicator, the New York Stock Exchange TRIN indicator, and the NASDAQ TRIN indicator. Now, that sounds like a lot, but it really isn't. We will talk about them fairly briefly. This is not a book on market timing. We use market timing for the purpose of enhancing the entries to the strategies I am going to show you. You can get into a lot more detail on the topic of market timing. As a matter of fact, entire books can be, and have been, written on the subject. I will not be as thorough as this subject actually deserves, but understand these market timing tools are very important.

The ones I am going to show you are the most effective. You may be wondering why we like to time entries with the market. Or for that matter, why not just play the market itself? These questions really do get to the heart of many of the issues that arise for traders.

First, we need to understand the concept of how the market affects individual stocks. Since we are about to broach this topic, how about an understanding of exactly what the market is.

What is the "Market?"

The "market" generally means the whole stock market. The problem is that there is no consensus as to what is included in the stock market, nor has anyone ever tried to quote the market as a whole. So we usually break the market apart in different ways. There are three main exchanges that trade the vast majority of all stocks.

They are the New York Stock Exchange (NYSE), the NASDAQ Stock Exchange (NASDAQ), and the American Stock Exchange (AMEX). While the numbers change, the NASDAQ is the largest with about 3,300 stocks trading. The NYSE is next with about 2,700, and the AMEX last with about 800.

It is more common, however, to view the market through the eyes of an index. This is a list of the larger, key stocks that are thought to be representative of the market itself. Some indexes you might have heard of are the S&P 500, the NASDAQ 100, and the Dow Industrials (Dow).

The S&P 500 is widely regarded as the best single gauge of the U.S. equities (stock) market. It is a representative sample of 500 companies in leading industries of the U.S. economy. Although the S&P 500 focuses on the large-cap segment of the market, with more than 80% coverage of U.S. equities, it is also an ideal proxy for the total market. To view the actual price and chart of the S&P 500, you put in the symbol for the cash index. For example, on many charting platforms, the symbol is $INX.X. or INX.

> The S&P 500 is widely regarded as the best single gauge of the U.S. equities (stock) market.

The NASDAQ 100 Index includes 100 of the largest domestic and international non-financial companies listed on the NASDAQ Stock Market, based on market capitalization. The NASDAQ 100 Index reflects companies across major industry groups, including computer hardware and software, telecommunications, retail/wholesale trade, and biotechnology. To view the actual price and chart of the NASDAQ 100, you put in the symbol for the cash index. For example, on many charting platforms the symbol is $NDX.X. or NDX.

The DOW Industrials is an index of only 30 stocks that is thought to be a cross section of our entire market. It is often used as the representative of the U.S. Market globally, and it is maintained and reviewed by editors of The Wall Street Journal. For the sake of continuity, composition changes are rare, and generally occur only after corporate acquisitions or other dramatic shifts in a component's core business. To view the actual price and chart of the DOW, you put in the symbol for the cash index. For example, on many charting platforms, the symbol is $DJI. or DJI. Note that there can be overlap. Intel Corp. (INTC), for example, is in the NASDAQ 100, S&P 500, and the Dow.

> While the Dow Industrials are often used to represent the U.S. equity market, remember it is a small index that is run like a mutual fund (stocks are added and removed on a subjective basis) and is not truly indicative of what the whole market may be doing.

Now, I don't want to make things more confusing, but there are a lot of other terms you will hear thrown around in the market. There are other vehicles used to view the above cross-section of the market. For example, there are also HOLDRS and ETFs, which are often confused. HOLDRS (spelled correctly even though it is pronounced as "holders") is an acronym for HOLding Company Depositary ReceiptS and are service marks of Merrill Lynch & Co., Inc. They are securities that represent an investor's ownership in the common stock or American Depositary Receipts of specified companies in a particular industry, sector, or group. In other words, they are traded like a single stock but represent ownership in several stocks in a sector in most cases. Common HOLDRS that traders use are BBH for the Biotech sector and HHH for the Internet sector.

ETF is an acronym for Exchange Traded Fund. Each ETF is a basket of securities designed to generally track an index (stock or bond, stock industry sector, or international stock), yet it trades like a single stock. There are more than 120 ETFs, and the most common ones traders use are the QQQ, SPY, and DIA. These are the ETFs for the NASDAQ 100, S&P 500, and Dow Industrials.

> HOLDRS and ETFs allow you to buy an entire sector or index as easy as buying a single stock without any restrictions.

In addition to the above, there are also futures. A futures contract is an obligation to receive or deliver a commodity or financial instrument sometime in the future, but at a price that's agreed upon today. People commonly think of futures in corn and pork bellies. But futures have also been developed for financial markets. As you might guess, there are futures for the NASDAQ 100, S&P 500, and the Dow. On many charting platforms, the symbols are /NDH6, /SPH6, and /ZDH6, respectively. By the way, the S&P Futures is the one that carries the nickname "spoos", if you have ever heard that term. Note, the last characters (H) represent the month and year of the future and change every quarter.

The most popular financial futures contracts were set up as new trading instruments by reducing their size. This set up a series of products known as the E-minis. They are available for the NASDAQ 100, S&P 500, and the Dow. Their symbols are /NQH6, /ESH6, and /YMH6 respectively. They are popular due to the reduced size and requirements.

So, how many ways could you view the S&P 500? Well, there is the cash index ($INX.X), the Electronically Traded Fund (SPY), the future (/SPH6), and the E-mini future (/ESH6). Is there any difference in the chart patterns? Well, they are all tied to the same underlying instrument, the price action of the S&P 500, so at the end of the day the chart patterns will all be similar. However, depending on what is happening in the market, the intraday price action may vary slightly as one of these may begin to move ahead of the others.

Microtrading in Relation to the Broader Market

So now we know what the market is. The next issue to understand is how the market affects our microtrading tactics. The market is the sum of all the individual stocks. However, not all individual stocks move the same. When the market moves, it takes about 80% of all stocks along with it. Or in other words, only about 80% of the stocks actually move in a consistent manner with the broader market. Some stocks are in sectors that traditionally move against the market, or simply follow their own pattern regardless of market. For example, gold and precious metal stocks historically have moved counter to the market, and often simply move irrespective of the market. Oil stocks are another excellent example of a sector that moves on its own. Depending upon the current economic environment, sectors such as defense stocks, cyclicals, and others may move on their own without regard to the broader market.

> About 80% of the stocks commonly traded will move and be influenced by the market in general.

Often, an individual stock may go on its own simply because of a shocking news story or financial announcement. You will see examples of this every day. The main point of all this is, despite these exceptions, 80% of the stocks will generally move with the broader market. It is known as "a rising tide lifts all boats."

When microtrading, we are dealing in a smaller time frame in which stocks may temporarily move in inconsistent directions. The astute microtrader needs to make sure stocks are being played in the direction of the broader market. For example, it would be highly unlikely to make a successful trade by going long KLAC (KLA-Tencor Co., a big name high tech stock) if the NASDAQ stock market was falling. It is not impossible, but it is highly unlikely. KLAC is a semiconductor stock, and it would be very unlikely for that sector to not be moving with the market. The only possibility is if KLAC had a very positive news announcement or positive financial numbers released.

The most common way for a microtrader to view the market is through the use of the S&P Futures Contract and the NASDAQ Futures Contract. Sometimes you may see the futures contracts move before the cash market because of the way big institutions purchase and unwind large positions. So our first market timing tools are going to be these two futures contracts. They represent futures positions on the vast majority of all the stocks traded in the marketplace.

> The astute player will stay on the side of the market the vast majority of the time—deviating only on special select situations.

We always view the futures contract through the eyes of a 2-minute window. In Figure 10.1, we are looking at a 2-minute chart of the S&P Futures Contract. Our chart for the futures contract looks the same as any other chart we use in microtrading. The only difference is that futures charts do not display volume information. We look at the futures on a candlestick chart and also notice we have our 20- and 200-period moving averages in place as we would on any other chart.

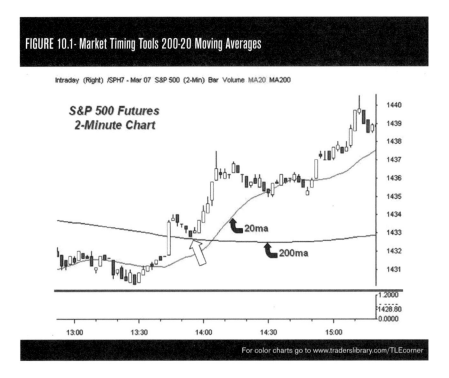

FIGURE 10.1- Market Timing Tools 200-20 Moving Averages

Intraday (Right) /SPH7 - Mar 07 S&P 500 (2-Min) Bar Volume MA20 MA200

S&P 500 Futures
2-Minute Chart

20ma

200ma

For color charts go to www.traderslibrary.com/TLEcorner

One way to display volume readings for the market is to view the market through the eyes of the QQQQ (the NASDAQ 100 tracking stock) or the SPY (the S&P 500 tracking stock). The tracking stocks will display volume information for its symbol; this is often an approximation of the actual market volume.

Take a look at what is happening on Figure 10.1. To the left of this chart, the market had been in a sideways downtrend. It hit its low at 1:30 p.m., which happens to be a micro reversal time, so that is not surprising. We'll discuss this phenomenon later.

However, I want you to notice that, as the futures came off the low, the rally was able to break right through the flat 200-period moving average. As you have just learned, it is unusual to be able to do this on the first effort. Notice that the bar that broke through the moving average is a huge white bar. We know that something definite has happened in the marketplace, and this is a very strong move. Notice the beautiful play as the market pulls back and bounces off the 200-period moving average (big arrow) and stays in an uptrend the rest of the day. The market itself could be played long at the arrow, and we know that we now have a bullish intraday bias for any other micro strategies we're looking at.

Once the 200-period moving average is clearly broken, there is a high probability of a continued move in that new direction.

Now, it doesn't mean that a trade can't be taken on the long side if the S&P Futures Contract and the NASDAQ Futures Contract are not rising. But it does say that you have some form of conflict. You need to understand what that means. You had better be in a stock that is expected to move against the market because of the sector it is in or you had better be playing a stock that is totally on its own for the day. Otherwise, you need to understand that there is a conflict that is lowering the odds of your trade working out. The astute trader tries to time longs when both futures contracts are rising, and time shorts when both futures contracts are declining.

Should You Play the Market Itself?

In the previous paragraph, I alluded to the concept of actually playing the market itself as a strategy. There are various ways that you can actually play the market to rally or fall. It can be played through any of the vehicles I mentioned earlier in this chapter. For example, if you wanted to be long the S&P 500 stocks, you could buy the SPY as you would any single stock. You can also be long S&P Futures Contracts or the S&P E-mini Futures Contract.

However, just because you know how to buy and sell the market does not mean you should do it. There are advantages and disadvantages of playing the market as opposed to playing individual stocks. Many people make their living playing the market; others wouldn't bother. Many will do both, depending upon what is set up the best. Let's take a look at that decision.

There are some advantages to trading the market itself. First and foremost is simplicity. You are trading one basic unit—the market. It allows you to focus without being distracted. There is also the very important advantage of consistency. When you trade the market, it is always high volume and easy to enter and exit trades. There are no surprises so there is little slippage to add to your expenses. You also eliminate some of the risk of having large moves go against you, as can happen in individual stocks when they gap overnight, or if they get halted intraday.

> Slippage is the difference between where you attempt to enter or exit a position and where you actually get filled. If you play low-volume stocks that tend to be very erratic, slippage costs can be enormous.

There are some disadvantages to only trading the market. First, it requires extreme patience and discipline. You are trading only one issue, and you may need to wait a long time for your particular setup to occur. The larger the time frame you trade, the more difficult it is to wait. For example, if you are a swing trader and choose to play only the market, you may have a setup one or two times a month. If you are a microtrader on a 2-minute chart, you may have multiple setups in a single day. By contrast, when you have a variety of individual stocks on your watch list, you are more likely to have a variety of setups forming. The bigger the variety of stocks, the better the chance of finding a play that works for you.

> There are advantages and disadvantages to playing the market as a strategy. Understanding these differences and finding your comfort level is important before risking any money on live trades.

Another disadvantage of playing only the market—and perhaps the biggest disadvantage—is what we're discussing in this section right now. When trading individual stocks, we can use the market as a guide to give us the edge as to the intraday direction of most stocks. We're also able to get a feel for the relative strength of the stock as compared to the market. When you trade the market, what is your guide? When you trade the market, what is the meaning of relative strength? This is the type of information you have to have in order to be successful.

New York Stock Exchange and NASDAQ TICK Indicators

Let's take a look at our next series of market timing indicators. They are the New York Stock Exchange and NASDAQ TICK indicators.

The TICK indicator measurement is done on the stocks on a given exchange. For example, let's look at the New York Stock Exchange. The New York TICK measures the number of stocks in the New York Stock Exchange at any moment in time trading on an uptick versus those trading on a downtick. If you have a New York Stock Exchange TICK reading of +300, it means that the number of stocks at this moment in time trading on an uptick outnumbered the stocks trading on a downtick by 300. If you have a reading of negative 600, it means that the stocks on the New York Stock Exchange trading on a downtick at this moment in time outnumber those that are trading on an uptick by 600.

> Trading on an uptick means that the price executed on the last trade was at least one penny higher than the price executed on the prior trade. The reverse is true for a downtick.

Figure 10.2 is a New York Stock Exchange TICK indicator and a NASDAQ TICK indicator. The TICK indicators have a twofold purpose. First, they give us an indication of bullishness or bearishness in the market at that particular time. Here are some of the rules the astute microtrader will follow when using the TICK indicator to his advantage: If the midpoint of the range in the ticks is above zero, it is generally bullish. If it is below zero, it is bearish.

Look at this chart from open until about 11:30 a.m. The ticks very consistently stalled at +1,000. A drop found support very consistently at a reading of about -200. The midpoint of these two readings is around +400. That is well above zero and, therefore, it's a bullish indication for the morning on this date. Another way to read the TICK for bullish or bearishness is if it has higher highs and higher lows. In Figure 10.2, we can see we made a significantly lower high (top arrow), which led to a much lower low. The following two rallies and two declines also formed lower highs and lower lows. This is a bearish indication.

So, we want to see where we find support and resistance, and if we are trending up or trending down. This is known as a "market internal," because it helps us to determine either a bullish or bearish bias for that time period. It gives us information beyond the price of the stock or the market.

FIGURE 10.2- Market Timing Tools

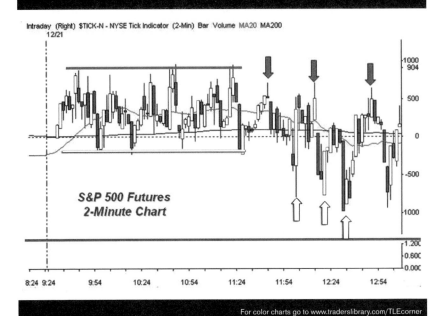

Intraday (Right) $TICK-N - NYSE Tick Indicator (2-Min) Bar Volume MA20 MA200
12/21

S&P 500 Futures
2-Minute Chart

For color charts go to www.traderslibrary.com/TLEcorner

The second purpose of the TICK is where we will find its use as a market timing tool. Notice how it oscillates in a fairly consistent range throughout the day. Even when it is trending up or trending down, it usually stays in the channel. Look at the range in Figure 10.2 from the time the market opened until 11:30 a.m. There is a very consistent support and resistance area ranging between +1,000 and -200. The concept here is to look to enter long positions in strong stocks when the TICK hits its low in the channel.

Likewise, the astute microtrader looks to short only when the TICK is coming off the highs of the channel. You are fighting the odds to enter a long position when the TICK is at +1,000, as shown in Figure 10.2.

> Astute microtraders will look to time all of their entries to coordinate with either the New York TICK or the NASDAQ TICK to increase the odds of every trade.

New York Stock Exchange and the NASDAQ TRIN Indicator

Last, but certainly not least, is the New York Stock Exchange and the NASDAQ TRIN indicator. It is also known as the ARMS index, named after its creator, Richard Arms, who developed the formula in 1967. It has also been called the Short Term Trading Index and the Trading Index (hence the acronym TRIN). We use the TRIN for the New York Exchange (symbol usually $TRIN-N), and for the NASDAQ Exchange (symbol usually $TRIN-Q).

The formula for the TRIN is below. If the advance/decline ratio is greater than the advancing volume/declining volume ratio, this means the volume on the sell side is greater, which is bearish. This will produce a TRIN number greater than 1.0, which means that

The TRIN a.k.a The ARMS Index

$$\frac{\text{advancing issues} / \text{declining issues}}{\text{advancing volume} / \text{declining volume}}$$

A rising TRIN means rising risk to longs

the TRIN works in an inverse fashion. As the TRIN rises, more volume is coming in to each sell on average, which has bearish implications.

A TRIN of exactly one is neutral. It means that the volume coming into the buys and sells is the same. A falling TRIN shows that the volume on the buy side is increasing, and this has bullish implications.

Now you have the formula that is readily available on literally hundreds and hundreds of websites, and certainly hundreds of books. Memorizing that formula does not make you a microtrader. As a matter of fact, there are probably many successful microtraders who could not reproduce that formula for you, but they know how to use it.

> The TRIN readings can be used as a gauge to confirm the trend of the market and as a timing tool to enter trades in either direction.

The TRIN can be used in several ways. When going long the market, we would like the TRIN to be below 1.0, and ideally below 0.8. When going short, we would like the TRIN above 1.0, and ideally above 1.2. We also look at the TRIN on a graph and apply all the concepts of Japanese candlestick charting: support, resistance, and moving averages. We look at the trend of the TRIN to see if it is confirming moves in the market (remember to confirm, it must move in an inverse fashion). The trend of the TRIN can often be the most important. For example, a TRIN of 0.7 may be bullish as an absolute number, but if the trend has been a nice, steady up-trend, the overall picture might be bearish.

Also the TRIN can be used as an overbought-oversold indicator. It is difficult to maintain readings of 0.3 or lower for a long period of time, especially after a bullish run has already happened in the market. Consider selling short-term long positions when the market shows signs of weakness after the TRIN has been at 0.3 or lower for a period of time. Likewise, it is difficult to maintain readings of 2.5 or higher for a long period of time, especially after a bearish run has already happened in the market. Consider covering short-term short positions when the market shows signs of strength after the TRIN has been at 2.5 or higher for a period of time. There are also uses on a bigger time frame for the swing trader. When the 10-day moving average of the TRIN gets above 1.2, it is likely a good area to cover shorts at the next sign of strength. Likewise, when the 10-day moving average of the TRIN gets below 0.8, look to take profits on longs at the next sign of weakness.

So, in essence, the microtrader attempts to time his or her longs when the TRIN indicators are declining. A rise in the TRIN equals a rise in risk; declining TRIN equals declining risks. Over 1.0 is bearish, and under 1.0 is bullish, but you need to look at both together. Also, understand that the opening minutes of the market are wild, and the opening 5 or more minutes of TRIN readings should be discarded.

In Figure 10.3, we can see both of these criteria coming together to form a very bullish bias. The TRIN opens a little above 1.0 and

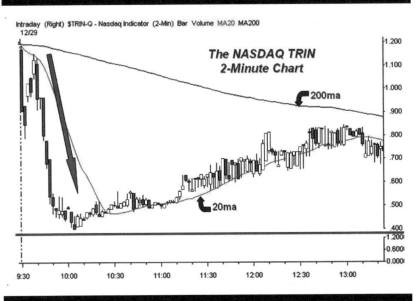

FIGURE 10.3- Market Timing Tools NASDAQ TRIN 2-min.

Intraday (Right) $TRIN-Q - Nasdaq Indicator (2-Min) Bar Volume MA20 MA200
12/29

**The NASDAQ TRIN
2-Minute Chart**

200ma

20ma

9:30   10:00   10:30   11:00   11:30   12:00   12:30   13:00

For color charts go to www.traderslibrary.com/TLEcorner

during the opening 5 minutes, it falls and rallies back to the opening price. Shortly after that it drops below 1.0, below the prior low set during the first 5 minutes, and begins a serious downtrend. All of these actions are very bullish for the market.

Figure 10.4 shows the price action of the NASDAQ market during the same time on the same day. You can see the sharp decline in the TRIN formed a strong rally in the NASDAQ market that morning. The TRIN, which fell below 1.0, preceded the market move above the high of the day, which led to the strong rally for the next 30 minutes. Astute microtraders should be aggressive on a

FIGURE 10.4- Market Timing Tools NASDAQ 100 (QQQQ)

Intraday (Right) QQQQ - NASDAQ 100 TR UNIT SER 1 (2-Min) Bar Volume MA20 MA200
12/29

**The NASDAQ 100 (QQQQ)
2-Minute Chart**

20ma

200ma

43.60
43.55
43.50
43.45
43.40
43.35
43.30
43.25
43.20
43.16
43.10
-1000000

9:30 10:00 10:30 11:00 11:30 12:00 12:30 13:00

For color charts go to www.traderslibrary.com/TLEcorner

bullish market setup when the TRIN confirms this action by dropping sharply.

The Three Phases to Every Trading Day

As market timing tools, these next concepts are simple yet priceless. These are my concepts, and they have helped me get an edge as a microtrader for many years.

There are three parts, or three phases to every day. Phase one starts at 9:30, at the opening bell—9:30 EST—and ends around 11:15

> ## The Perfect Market Timing Scenario
>
> Let's take all of these market timing tools I have discussed and put them together to create a perfect microtrading situation. The perfect microtrading long scenario will exist when the NASDAQ and the S&P Futures Contract are positive and moving to the upside; when the New York Stock Exchange and the NASDAQ TICK indicator are in positive territory on average and rising, and when the New York Stock Exchange and the NASDAQ TRIN indicators are below 1.0 and declining. When all of that comes together, it creates the best scenario for the microtrader who is primarily biased on the long side. For the short side, we would want all of these conditions to be exactly reverse.

EST. In phase one, the microtrader is focused on trading breakouts and breakdowns and reversals. We will talk in great detail about those very shortly.

Phase two of the day starts at 11:15 and ends at 2:15. This 11:15 period to 2:15 period is called the midday doldrums. The midday doldrums is that black hole in the market, that time of day where virtually everything stops. The market goes dead. At least this is

> ## The 3 Micro Trading Phases of the Day
>
> **Phase 1** - 9:30 to 11:15 (Trade BO/Reversals)
>
> **Phase 2** - 11:15 to 2:15 (Mid-day Doldrums)
>
> **Phase 3** - 2:15 to 4:00 (Trade BO/Reversals)

true on most days. It is certainly a time where many traders give back a lot of money.

If the market was biased to the upside, the market either goes flat during this period or tapers off. If the market was biased to the downside during phase one, during phase two it will either start to drift higher or go flat. The midday doldrums period is that very dangerous time for most microtraders. We tell most microtraders to go to lunch because this is historically the flattest time of the day. There is a very good reason why this period lacks a great deal of excitement or volatility. It's simply because the majority of the big boys on Wall Street go to lunch.

I've spent a great deal of time down on Wall Street. I was an accountant as my first profession. But I was frustrated because of my dream to become an astute market player. I would take my brown bag lunch (I worked for a law firm on Wall Street in the accounting department), and I would go down and sit at the doorstep of JP Morgan, right down the street from where I worked. I'd watch the powerful players come out of the JP Morgan front doors. You could always spot a market maker, which is what I wanted to be. You could always spot these powerful players who walk with phenomenal confidence.

When I started to delve into the market and learn about some of the intraday tendencies, I learned how this excessive volatility in the first hour-and-a-half represents phenomenal microtrading opportunities. I also learned that at a certain time, the market just goes flat.

What's interesting about this time frame is that most market making desks are populated by two traders. There is one senior trader and one junior trader.

It's the senior trader who handles the institutional clients. When an institutional client calls the desk and says, "You know what John, I need 48,000 shares of ALTERA by the end of day today. You work it at your discretion," the senior market maker handles that order. This client is responsible for a lot of commissions and a lot of business to the firm. So, only the big man handles this order.

> The "doldrums" can be a difficult time for most traders unless you understand what you're doing. Most traders give back gains during lunch.

So, he is in the market working this 48,000 share position. He is buying a little, backing off, and knocking the stock back down. As he knocks the stock back down on the offer price, he's picking up some and socking it away, 5,000 here, 200 here, and 1,000 here, accumulating this 48,000 share position. He is jockeying back and forth. If the price gets a little too ahead of itself, he's not interested in buying for his client. He might even sell some to knock it back down before he buys more for his client. He is working the order.

But at 11:15, market makers have to eat. They go to lunch and leave the controls to the junior market makers who have absolutely no control, no authority to continue jockeying for the stock. They just maintain the market. You will find this prevalent, especially throughout almost all NASDAQ market making stocks and certainly a lot of the New York Stock Exchange and listed stocks as well.

During that time frame, breakouts will tend to fail because there is no follow-through in the market. Breakdowns in the market during the midday doldrums will begin their move a little bit, fake a lot of people out, and rally right back to the upside. Naturally, there are exceptions, but remember what I discussed earlier: trading is all about odds. The odds of follow-through decrease during lunch.

Phase three obviously completes our day. It starts at 2:15 and ends at the closing bell at 4:00 EST. The style of market play or the tactics used by the microtrader during phase three are breakouts, breakdowns, and reversals. One of the most reliable trading tactics I'm going to show you is exclusive to phase three.

Figure 10.5 shows an example of the three phases of the trading day. We are looking at a 5-minute chart of Research in Motion Limited (RIMM). I want you to note that the first move during phase one, 9:30 to 11:15 EST, is to the upside. Market makers are primarily in buy mode, jockeying for stock, driving it up, until the stomach starts growling. Now they call up their buddies and they go for a very long lunch. Around 2:15, 2:30 or so, the big man comes back, takes the controls, and continues the job he started in the beginning of the day.

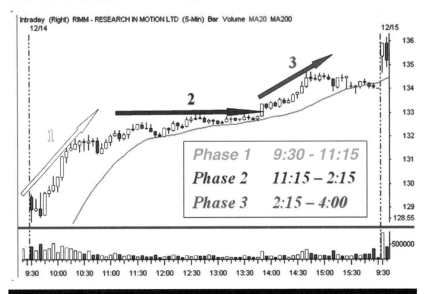

FIGURE 10.5- Market Timing Tools Phase 1-2-3 Upturn

Intraday (Right) RIMM - RESEARCH IN MOTION LTD (5-Min) Bar Volume MA20 MA200

Phase 1	9:30 - 11:15
Phase 2	11:15 – 2:15
Phase 3	2:15 – 4:00

For color charts go to www.traderslibrary.com/TLEcorner

Take a look at a variety of charts on your own charting platform. Look for these three phases of the trading day. Remember the times are approximate and should not be interpreted to the exact minute. You'll be amazed at how often stocks, or the market in general, trade in three distinct phases.

If you look at this chart during phase two, the midday doldrums, look how quiet the stock becomes. If you were trying to trade the stock during this time, you can see how difficult it would be. Right at 12:00, it looks like it is going to break down, then rallies. Then at 12:30, the stock breaks to a new high of the day, only to go nowhere for one-and-a-half hours. It isn't until the beginning of phase three that the stock finally finishes its move to the upside.

What's interesting is that move between phase two and phase three. We will build some very interesting trading tactics around this event because it happens over and over again. This is our clue that after lunch, the original move is going to continue.

Figure 10.6 is another example of the three phases of the trading day. We are looking at the stock Qualcomm Inc., (QCOM.) Here we have a totally different pattern, but I wanted to show you how the stock still obeys the three phases of the trading day. Here we

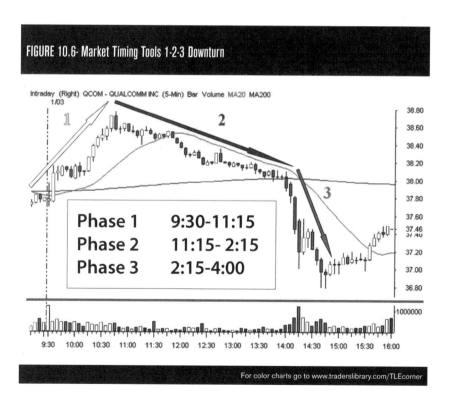

FIGURE 10.6- Market Timing Tools 1-2-3 Downturn

Intraday (Right) QCOM - QUALCOMM INC (5-Min) Bar Volume MA20 MA200
1/03

Phase 1   9:30-11:15
Phase 2   11:15- 2:15
Phase 3   2:15-4:00

have phase one rallying like before. Notice that while phase two is a low volume, quiet period with very low range of motion, the stock is constantly falling until it has given up all of the morning profits.

Now phase three takes off and we see a very sharp sell-off to the downside. Note the size of the black bars in phase three as compared to phase two. Notice phase three accelerates downward as the 200-period moving average is violated.

Why the difference in patterns? Well, not every day is exactly the same. Something happened to the stock this day, or something happened in the market. But the concept that gives us these odds is that the three phases of the day often follow like clockwork. In other words, once you determine an upward bias, it holds all through the first phase. Once you determine a downward bias, it holds all through the third phase. In both of these examples, phase two is difficult to trade because of the narrow trading range during the doldrums.

Micro Reversal Times

Now we begin a fascinating discussion about the nine micro reversal times. There are specific times, with specific cycles in the market, and this is one of the most amazing things about intraday market play.

I tell traders who are new to the market and do not understand reversal times that they are at such a disadvantage they should not even be trading. There are certain times of the day that produce incredibly consistent results, yet few people seem to recognize this power. When a stock is rallying or declining into one of these reversal times, it will reverse for no apparent reason on an incredibly consistent basis.

> Traders who are not aware of, or do not properly utilize, the micro reversal times throughout the trading day are at a big disadvantage.

These nine reversal times are as follows, and I have them broken up by the three phases. Again, all times are Eastern Standard.

Phase One Reversal Times

First is 9:35, only 5 minutes after the open. Early morning pre-market orders to buy and sell stocks at open give market makers and specialists a blank check to run stocks wildly during the opening of trading, only to reverse when the orders run out. Next is 10:00, a very, very powerful reversal time. I want you to highlight that one, circle it, and remember it. Next is the equally strong 10:30 reversal time. Last, but not least, we have the reversal time that separates phase one from phase two, 11:15. This marks the beginning of the doldrums.

Now, like with anything in trading, you can't be too exact with reversal times. They are a concept. The reversal often happens a little before 10:00, and a little after 10:00. You have to give it some leeway, but you will be amazed at how accurately and how frequently the market turns at these specific times. Generally the stock, or market, will react within one 5-minute bar of the reversal time.

> Reversal times are concepts, not exact moments in time. Like everything else in trading, when they come together with other events, they become all the more powerful.

Phase Two Reversal Times

These reversal times are two in number. The first one is at 12:00 noon, and the second, and most powerful, is 1:30. It's at these very powerful reversal times that we are going to design some microtrading strategies.

Phase Three Reversal Times

First is 2:15, a very powerful reversal time, which of course kicks off phase three. Then 3:00 is another very powerful reversal time. This revolves around the fact that the bond market closes at 3:00 EST. Last is the 3:30 reversal time.

Some of these reversal times have what appears to be some rationale behind them. Obviously, 11:15 and 2:15 are the beginning and ending of the doldrums. 9:35 and 10:00 have to do with overnight orders being filled and the power that market makers and specialists have during that time period.

As I mentioned, 3:00 is the close of the bond market. Depending upon the current economic conditions and whatever the talking heads on TV are worried about at the moment, the closing of the bond market may serve to be a bullish or bearish happening for the stock market. However, it is often the case that when the market is rallying into 3:00 and the bond market closes, it will often have the effect of reversing the stock market.

As for the rest of these times, there are some theories that may or may not be true. However, the rationale does not matter. What matters is that these times often have a significant influence on the

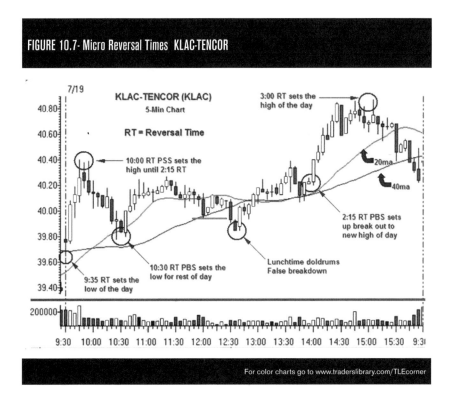

FIGURE 10.7- Micro Reversal Times KLAC-TENCOR

intraday pattern of the market. Go through your own charts and see for yourself. You will likely never trade intraday again without timing your strategy to one of the key micro reversal times.

Take a look at Figure 10.7. This is a 5-minute chart of KLA Tencor (KLAC). Remember, every bar represents 5 minutes of trading and this chart covers one trading day. This chart does not have the 200-period moving average because it was off the chart.

Notice the areas identified on the chart. The 9:35 reversal time sets the low of the day. The stock opened and ran down sharply during the opening minutes of trading. It immediately rebounded and that low set during the opening minutes turned out to be the low for the entire day. This is not an unusual event.

> It will not be long before you will be building your intraday strategies around the micro reversal times.

Next the Pristine Sell Setup that occurs at 10:00 sets a high of the day that lasts until 2:15. It is not uncommon for traders to purchase during the first 5 minutes and sell into the 10:00 reversal time. Notice the topping tails that form right at 10:00 after a multiple bar rally to that area. The drop this produces continues for seven 5-minute bars until a big bottoming tail forms right into the 10:30 reversal time. This 10:30 low becomes the low for the rest of the trading day.

Notice that the lunchtime doldrums delivers a false breakdown, which is exactly what an astute trader should expect. That leads to a slow rally that challenges the high of the day. The pullback from that rally, now out of the doldrums, sets up a Pristine Buy Setup at 2:15 reversal time. This leads to a powerful breakout, and a new high of the day. Naturally, that rally ends at 3:00 reversal time with a large topping tail, which marks the high of the day. The high of the day, the low of the day, the two next biggest pivots, and the best buy setup all happened at reversal times.

I did not look long or hard to find this chart. Check it out for yourself. Pull up your favorite charts or the market itself and notice the times listed above. It is not that every reversal time will have a major market move, but notice the major pivots, and the highs and lows in a stock's price every day. You will be amazed how often these major moves happen at or within one 5-minute bar of a reversal time.

The importance of the various times may change some in different market environments, and every reversal time is not affected every day. But if you time your strategies with key reversal times, they will be all the more effective.

How to Use Micro Reversal Times

So you may be wondering if the intraday micro reversal times work on the market or just on select stocks. The answer is the same as is with most everything in trading. They apply to the market just

FIGURE 10.8- Micro Reversal Times SDDR TR

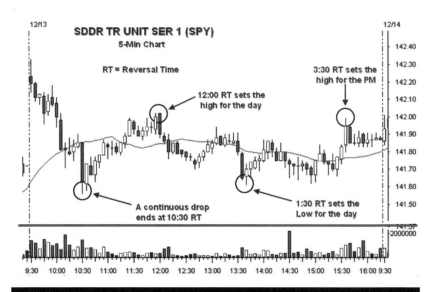

SDDR TR UNIT SER 1 (SPY)
5-Min Chart

RT = Reversal Time

12:00 RT sets the
high for the day

3:30 RT sets the
high for the PM

A continuous drop
ends at 10:30 RT

1:30 RT sets the
Low for the day

For color charts go to www.traderslibrary.com/TLEcorner

as well as they apply to any individual stock. Figure 10.8 is an example of how the reversal times apply to the broadest measure of market that we use.

This is a 5-minute chart of the SPY. Remember that the SPY is the tracking stock for the S&P 500. The market (SPY) opened strong on this day but sold off hard from the open. Several times it looked like it wanted to rally, but it wasn't until the widest bar on the chart dropped right into the 10:30 reversal time. This set a low for the day. Notice that many experienced traders may have been looking to short the lower part of this black bar. This is because the lower part of this bar trades under the low of the day, and trades under the area gap that happened in the morning. However, the astute microtrader knows to assume that when the market has moved in one direction for one hour and when a reversal time is near, then a reversal will be at hand.

Like most all trading tactics, the micro reversal times apply to any stock, or to the market itself.

The rally off the lows continues until 12:00 noon precisely. Noon ends up being a high for the rest of the day. The market drops throughout the doldrums until the widest bar of the fall takes us into the 1:30 reversal time. The stock then rallies above the afternoon consolidation but stalls into the 3:00 reversal time.

Another way to look at Figure 10.8 is to look at the two highest and two lowest points on the chart after the market opened. All of these major reversal points were at micro reversal times. Again, this is the market itself we are reviewing.

When you go into the market and find these examples, you will quickly believe the power of the micro reversal times and you likely will begin to build your trading strategies around them.

Self-test questions

1. Which of the following is NOT considered a market timing tool?

   a. The NASDAQ futures contract.
   b. The New York Stock Exchange TRIN indicator.
   c. The Dow Jones Industrial Average advance/decline ratio.
   d. The S&P 500 TICK indicator.

2. Microtraders often use Exchange Traded Funds (ETFs) rather than individual stocks because it enables them to do what?

   a. Trade a specific segment of the overall market as represented by a specific index, such as the NASDAQ 100.
   b. Avoid some of the volatility associated with many individual stocks.
   c. Reduce the fees associated with trades of individual shares.
   d. Eliminate the need to pick out one or two individual winners from among the thousands of listed stocks.

3. When the TICK indicator for a given market exchange reads +300, it means what?

    a. 300 stocks have traded during the most recent tracking period.

    b. 300 of the stocks listed on the exchange have a "buy" recommendation from analysts.

    c. There are 300 more listed stocks trading higher at the moment than there are stocks trading lower.

    d. There are 300 seconds remaining until the exchange closes for the day.

4. The Trading Index, or TRIN, compares the relationship between rising and falling prices and rising and falling volume. Which of the following statements about TRIN readings is incorrect?

    a. A TRIN of exactly 1.00 is neutral.

    b. A falling TRIN shows that buy side volume is increasing and is bullish.

    c. A rising TRIN shows that sell side volume is rising, which is bearish.

    d. A TRIN number greater than 1.00 is bullish, while a TRIN below 1.00 is bearish.

5. Microtraders break each market day down into three phases, actively looking to trade breakouts and reversals during which phases?

   a. Phases 1 (9:30 to 11:15) and 2 (11:15 to 2:15).
   b. Phases 1 (9:30 to 11:15) and 3 (2:15 to 4:00).
   c. Phases 2 (11:15 to 2:15) and 3 (2:15 to 4:00).
   d. Phase 2 (11:15 to 2:15) only.

For answers, go to www.traderslibrary.com/TLEcorner

Chapter 11

Tactics for Phase One

Up until this point, we have been discussing all the tools needed for microtrading. We have come to understand the various types of trading and what our role is as a microtrader. We have seen the tools we will need, and have become acquainted with various market timing tools that help us initiate trades at the highest probable time. We have just learned that the market is going to aid us by giving us specific times of day when our trades will be most likely to be successful. It is now time to learn the actual tactics we will use to enter our microtrades.

We will begin by discussing the micro tactics that are most effective in phase one. As you remember, phase one is the time from 9:30 until 11:15 EST. We have five tactics to exploit these reversal time frames during the first phase of the day. Figure 11.1 lists the five phase one trading tactics for your reference.

FIGURE 11.1- Micro Trading Phase 1

Phase 1 Trading Tactics

1) The 9:30 Breakout/Breakdown Play

2) The 10:00 Reversal Play

3) Pristine's 30-Minute Rule

4) The 11:00 Topping/Bottoming Play

5) The 200 Moving Average Play

For color charts go to www.traderslibrary.com/TLEcorner

FIGURE 11.2- 9:35 BD, 10:00 Bottom

For color charts go to www.traderslibrary.com/TLEcorner

The first tactic is called the 9:35 breakout or breakdown play. Figure 11.2 is a 5-minute chart of Veritas Software Inc. I want you to note that during the first 5 minutes of the trading day, the microtrader is on the edge of his or her seat watching his or her collection of stocks very carefully without any action.

The microtrader understands that the first 5 minutes call for no action, according to our philosophy. It calls for watching those stocks that gap up or gap down. What I have found is that stocks will often reveal their true trend for the day after the first five minutes.

A stock that opens at 9:30 at a significantly higher or lower price than it closed at 4:00 the previous session is said to have "gapped." Gapping stocks can present excellent trading opportunities to the microtrader.

We determine what direction to play by whether the stock trades above the first 5 minutes of the trading day, or below the first 5 minutes of the trading day. If the stock trades above the first 5 minutes of trading, many microtraders enter the stock long with the idea that the stock will run up right into 10:00.

If after the first minutes of trading, as was the case with VRTS, the stock breaks below the low established during that 5-minute period, many microtraders will short the stock with the idea that the first move of the day will be to the downside right into the 10:00 reversal time frame.

So, the microtrader wants to try to capitalize on a 15- or maybe 20-minute move after the first 5 minutes of the trading day. The goal is to capture the move into the second reversal time, 10:00. So, after 5 minutes, the microtrader is going to mark off a high established in the first 5 minutes of trading. He or she is going to mark off the low established in the first 5 minutes of trading, and then see which way the stock breaks.

This is very important. Not all trades work out as we like, and the losses must be limited. So every tactic I show you will have a protective stop loss built into it. It is the mark of a loser to trade without a stop or to ignore stops once set.

> The No. 1 reason for traders to have to quit trading is the refusal to set or take protective stop losses.

For this tactic, if the stock breaks upward, I am going to go long with the protective stop placed below the low of the first 5-minute bar. The idea is that the breakout above the first 5-minute high will rally right into 10:00. If it does not, I am out for a small loss.

If the stock breaks below the low established during the first 5 minutes of trading, the assumption is that it will drop all the way back into 10:00. So, the object is to take advantage of this micromove by shorting the stock and at the same time, placing a protective stop over the first 5 minute bar's high.

In this case, VRTS opens up with a gap down and established its first 5-minute high and low. The next 5-minute period is a pause; the third 5-minute period cracks the low. This is the first bar that violates the high or low of the first 5-minute bar.

In this case, the microtrader will attempt to get short as the stock breaks the 5-minute low. As you can see, the stock drops over the next 15 or 20 minutes all the way into 10:00. It is no surprise that VTRS bottoms exactly at the 10:00 reversal time.

At 10:00, the stock has moved down into the 10:00 period. The microtrader, having profited from the downside, will often attempt to trade the stock above the last black bar around 10:00 with the idea that the next rally is going to continue right into the 10:30 reversal.

If you look at Figure 11.2, the stock bottomed at 10:00. The aggressive microtrader understanding that 10:00 does typically produce major reversals, would attempt to go long this stock above the last black bar with the idea of the stock rallying right into 10:30. This is the 10:00 reversal play. Notice the stock rallies right to the declining 20-period moving average and right at the 10:30 reversal time.

Figure 11.3 is another example of the 9:35 breakdown strategy and the 10:00 reversal play. Network Appliance (NTAP) gaps to the downside. The microtrader does nothing at the open. The microtrader lets the stock trade for a full 5 minutes with no activity. After 5 minutes, the microtrader marks off the high and marks off the low.

As we see on this chart, the next 5-minute bar violates the low established during the first 5 minutes of trading. That microtrader attempts to get short with the idea that the stock will drop all the way into the 10:00 period.

Once the microtrader gets short, he attempts to cover his position right into the 10:00 reversal period, understanding that the 10:00

FIGURE 11.3- 9:35 BD, 10:00 Bottom, 11:00 Top

is also a major reversal time. This microtrader, having now covered his or her short, attempts to go long above the last black bar, which would put the microtrader in the stock around $34. NTAP now rallies right into the 10:30 reversal time.

This is where we teach our traders to exit the trade. This stock rallies right into the next reversal period. It also happens to coincide with a retest of the opening price. Again, as we can see, the stock continued to move higher, but this is where we would encourage our traders to exit. Stocks can do most anything, but following the odds is what is important and the odds say the stock will stall at 10:30.

FIGURE 11.4- 9:35 BD, 10:00 Bottom, 11:00 Top (Close Trade)

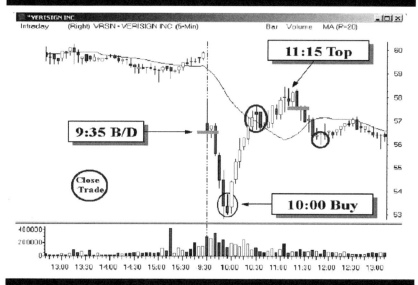

For color charts go to www.traderslibrary.com/TLEcorner

10:00 and 10:30 form powerful reversal times every day in many stocks, making for a variety of opportunities for the microtrader.

Now, what happens next is that this stock rallies right into the 11:00 hour. The aggressive microtrader, understanding that 11:00 to 11:15 is when market makers start getting hungry, would attempt to short this stock below the last white bar with the idea of covering somewhere around the 12:00 reversal. That is the 11:00 topping play.

In Figure 11.4, we have a 5-minute chart of VRSN. The same entry applies. The 5-minute low was violated; the stock drops right into

FIGURE 11.5- 30-min Buy, 11:00 Top (Immunex)

For color charts go to www.traderslibrary.com/TLEcorner

the 10:00 reversal period. After covering the short, the microtrader attempts to go long around the 10:00 time frame, if the drop went right into 10:00. This rally takes us right into the declining 20-period moving average, where the trader is instructed to sell. It is not only the declining 20-period moving average, but it is also the 10:30 reversal time and the area of the opening price.

Note that this micro-move topped out at 11:15. The aggressive trader would look to short below the last white bar with the idea of it dropping into the next reversal period. Again, on this chart you see examples of three of the five trading tactics for phase one. They are the 9:30 breakdown play, the 10:00 reversal play, and the 11:00 topping play.

Next is IMNX, Figure 11.5. What's interesting about this stock is that there was a dip below the 5-minute bar, but the stock failed to really drop and it buoyed right back to the upside. This is an indication the stock does not want to go down, and this is when the Pristine 30-minute rule comes into play.

> The more tactics to come together at one time, the better odds you'll have as a microtrader.

The 30-minute rule calls for us to follow the stock now that the 5-minute breakdown has failed. We now move to the 30-minute time frame. We let the stock trade for 30 minutes. After 30 minutes of trading, we mark the high established during the 30-minute period. And, if the stock manages to break above the high established in the first 30 minutes of the day, we look for the stock to have a micro-move into the 11:00 or 11:15 reversal.

Note, again, that the exact intraday top of this move was at 11:15. The aggressive trader could attempt to go short the stock once it traded below the low of the last white bar, right into the next reversal period.

We have another example of the 30-minute buy tactic used on PHSY in Figure 11.6. Note that whenever I get equal highs throughout a 30-minute period, I'm going to mark those highs because a blastoff through those highs typically starts a very powerful

FIGURE 11.6- 30-min Buy, 11:00 Top (Pacific Health Systems)

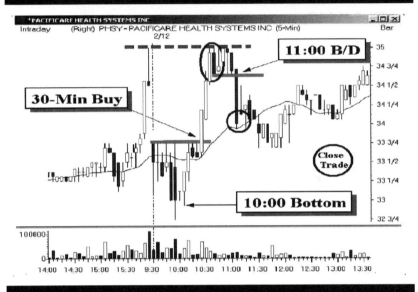

move. Whenever I have relatively equal highs for a full 30 minutes, it will form a small base and I'm going to use the Pristine 30-minute buy rule. I'm going to mark the high established during the first 30 minutes of trading and buy the breakout above those highs. I will be looking for a rally right into the 11:15 reversal.

> When a stock consolidates in a narrow range before trading above its 30-minute high or low, it is likely to continue in that direction.

Note that this stock gapped down on the current day after forming a high late the prior day. This rally goes right back to that prior

FIGURE 11.7- 10:00 Top, 10:30 Reversal

high, which is where we would instruct our microtraders to sell. This breakdown happens to be around 11:00. The stock pulls back all the way to the rising 20-period moving average. The aggressive microtrader would attempt to go short the 11:00 high and cover into the rising 20-period moving average.

In Figure 11.7, we see TER get up and rally into the 10:00 reversal time. It gets extended from the rising 20-period moving average and forms a topping tail. The microtrader shorts underneath the low of the topping tail bar with the expectation of covering into the 10:30 reversal time. The setup at 10:30 is not only good for covering the short, but is also a 10:30 reversal time with a narrow bar to play long. Remember, your stop is going to be underneath the low of the decline, which means the long play at 10:00 will be very, very tight.

Finally, we have the last of the phase one trading tactics, the 200-period moving average play. This micro tactic is using the 15-minute chart, not a 5-minute chart. Note that we are looking at several days on a 15-minute chart, and the days are separated by vertical dotted lines. Note the high on Figure 11.8, which was established in the early part of the following day, and the severe decline. The next day, the stock rallies to retest that high and, at the same time,

FIGURE 11.8- 200 MA Play at 10:30 Reversal

For color charts go to www.traderslibrary.com/TLEcorner

retested the declining 200-period moving average. When you see prior price resistance in the area of the 200-period moving average, rallies into that area make excellent shorts. The stock drops all the way back down to the prior lows.

As you can see, the astute microtrader looks for combinations of these tactics where possible. For example, when the stock rallies into the 10:30 reversal period near a prior high, and at a declining 200-period moving average, the aggressive microtrader would attempt to go short below the low of the last 15-minute bar.

1. Which of the following is NOT a Phase 1 trading tactic?

    a. The 9:30 Breakout/Breakdown Play.

    b. The 10:00 Reversal Play.

    c. The 10:30 Recovery Play.

    d. The 11:00 Topping/Bottoming Play.

2. The author has found that stocks will often reveal their true trend for the day after how long?

    a. The first five minutes.

    b. The first 15 minutes.

    c. The first half hour.

    d. The first hour.

3. The Pristine 30-Minute Rule applies when:

    a. A stock has not made any kind of opening move in the first 30 minutes of the trading day.

    b. A stock has tried to break out or break down below the high or low set during the first five minutes, but has failed, reversing and moving in the opposite direction.

    c. A stock moved in one direction for the final 30 minutes of the prior day, but reversed at today's opening.

    d. News forces a delay in a stock's opening for at least 30 minutes.

4. The No. 1 reason traders have to quit trading is:

    a. The lack of sufficient time to track the market and identify opportunities.

    b. Failure to develop the skills needed to identify key entry signals.

    c. Lack of a good computerized screening system.

    d. The refusal to set or adhere to appropriate protective stops.

5. The last of the Phase 1 microtrading tactics calls for using what?

    a. A 5-minute, 20-period moving average chart.

    b. A 5-minute, 200-period moving average chart.

    c. A 15-minute, 200-period moving average chart.

    d. An 15-minute chart with trendlines connecting both highs and lows.

For answers, go to www.traderslibrary.com/TLEcorner

Chapter 12

Tactics for Phase Two

Let's talk about phase two trading tactics. You may have noticed that in phase one, we primarily used the 5-minute time frame. That is because many of the moves were only expected to last 20 to 30 minutes, into the next reversal time. The reversal times are also relatively exact and nice entries can be found on the 5-minute chart.

In phase two, we primarily use the 15-minute time period. We want a larger time period because we want to be more sure of the plays in the midday doldrums. The strategies must be exact, and we do not want to over-trade, so we will use the slower but surer time frame afforded to us on the 15-minute chart.

There are several trading tactics we use with the 15-minute chart during phase two. You can see them listed in Figure 12.1. You may notice that one of the strategies has an unusual title. The reason is

FIGURE 12.1- Micro Trading Phase 2

Phase 2 Trading Tactics

1) The 11:00 – 11:15 Topping/Bottoming Play

2) The Good Lunch Play

3) The 15-minute Trading Dip Play

4) The 1:30 Reversal Play

For color charts go to www.traderslibrary.com/TLEcorner

simple. I want you to go to lunch too. That's right, that's the time of day that's precarious, so go to lunch.

If you take a look at YHOO in Figure 12.2, you will see something I have discussed a few times, but here is an excellent example of the concept. Look at how far away this 15-minute chart got from the rising 20-period moving average. The 20-period moving average is like the leash, and the stock price is like the dog. The dog can only run so far away, then the leash is going to pull the stock back in. And, if this rally or top happens to coincide around 11:00, the microtrader who understands this concept is all over the stock the instant it trades below the low of the last 15-minute bar.

Figure 12.3 is another 15-minute chart. Note that the prior day, the stock rallied to a 1:30 top, and that 1:30 happened to coincide

FIGURE 12.2- 11:00-11:15 Topping Play

FIGURE 12.2- 11:00-11:15 Topping Play

For color charts go to www.traderslibrary.com/TLEcorner

FIGURE 12.3- The 1:30 Reversal Play

For color charts go to www.traderslibrary.com/TLEcorner

with a declining 200-period moving average. This stock is doing nothing but going down the instant it trades below the low of the prior 15-minute bar. The next day, 1:30 proves once again to be a turning point. On the 15-minute chart, the stock drops right into 1:30 on a very hard drop. The stock is very extended from the declining 20-period moving average, the volume increases dramatically at the very bottom, and this is all happening into the 1:30 reversal time. The microtrader, understanding the 1:30 time frame reversal, would look to buy the stock the instant it traded above the high of the last 15-minute bar.

Figure 12.4 is an example of the 15-minute trading dip showing MCHP on a 15-minute chart. The stock rallies during the late

FIGURE 12.4- The 15-Minute Trading Dip

morning and peaks, but then has a 15-minute dip. This bottom is exactly at 1:30 reversal time. The trader, knowing the stock has dropped into 1:30, looks to buy the instant the stock trades above the high of the last 15-minute bar and rallies right into the 2:00 reversal time frame or the 2:15 time frame.

Figure 12.5 shows another excellent example of the 15-minute dip, as well as the 1:30 reversal. This is a 15-minute chart of Novelus (NVLS). The stock rallies to a new high on the day. It forms a double topping tail right at the 12:00 reversal time. The pullback begins and trades over a prior bar right at the 1:30 reversal time. It also is sitting on the prior highs, which is a form of support, and makes this trade even better. With a 15-minute drop into 1:30, I

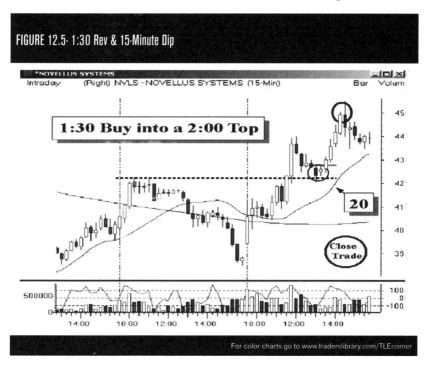

FIGURE 12.5- 1:30 Rev & 15-Minute Dip

am all over the stock the moment—the instant—the stock trades above the high of the last 15-minute bar. We get an explosion, and yes, you guessed it, right into 3:00.

> Remember: The average microtrader overstays his or her welcome during lunch. Play in the direction of the odds and remember the moves will likely be smaller.

Now again, let's discuss something very important. We're talking about taking trades during phase two that we have already identified as the doldrums. One of the biggest mistakes novice traders make is to overtrade this part of the day. These are very select plays at a very select time when the odds shift in your favor. It is during these times we have an edge. The other times, we don't know what's going to happen. It's like shooting from the hip. This is when it is best to read the paper or go to lunch.

Self-test questions

1. In monitoring for Phase Two tactics, microtraders generally use 15-minute charts because:

   a. The market tends to move more slowly during Phase Two of the trading day so the strategies must be more exact.

   b. We want to allow ourselves at least 15 minutes to get lunch between trades.

   c. Five-minute charts are too short to clearly illustrate prolonged moves.

   d. None of the above.

2. Many stocks show a tendency to make new highs around 11:00 a.m., so astute microtraders will do what?

   a. Buy the stock whenever that happens.

   b. Watch the stock closely and buy if it moves above that prior top.

   c. Sell the stock any time it makes a high around 11:00 a.m.

   d. Sell the stock if it subsequently trades below the low of the last 15-minute bar.

3. Microtraders tend to watch the relationship of a stock to its 20-period moving average because:

    a. The 20-period moving average is like the bell on a cow, signaling when a stock gets out of its usual pattern.
    b. The 20-period moving average tends to pull the stock back when it moves too far away, much as a leash pulls a dog back to its master.
    c. The 20-day moving average is better at marking tops or bottoms than a trendline.
    d. The 20-day moving average identifies reversals more quickly than a 10-period moving average.

4. Why is 1:30 p.m. such a key point in monitoring for Phase 2 tactics?

    a. Top market specialists are full from lunch and thus slower to react.
    b. The mid-day Doldrums tend to be at their worst at 1:30 p.m.
    c. 1:30 is frequently the point when stocks reverse their short-term midday trends.
    d. The direction of trading at 1:30 p.m. tends to be the direction stocks will take for the remainder of the day.

5. The reduction in volume as traders take their lunch breaks is the basis for which Phase Two tactic?

   a. The 1:30 Reversal Play.
   b. The 15-Minute Trading Dip Play.
   c. The 2:00 Top Play.
   d. The 20-Period Moving Average Play.

For answers, go to www.traderslibrary.com/TLEcorner

Chapter 13
Tactics for Phase Three

We are now ready for the last phase of the day. Here are our trading strategies as you see listed in Figure 13.1. The first is the 3:00 topping and bottoming play, which is similar to the 10:00 and the 1:30 topping and bottoming play except now it's 3:00. Again, we have the 200-period moving average play, which we've talked about already. Last, most certainly not least, the late day breakout play. Circle this one.

This late-day breakout play is the most important intraday microtrading tactic of all. It is the most reliable. If you have liked the results of some of these turning points, then you are going to be amazed as to how often the late day breakout and breakdown play will reward you.

FIGURE 13.1- Micro Trading Phase 3

Phase 3 Trading Tactics

1) The 3:00 Topping/Bottoming Play

2) 200 Moving Average Play

3) The Late Day Breakout/down Play

FIGURE 13.2- 3:00 Topping Play

Figure 13.2 is an example of the 3:00 top into the close. The stock on the 15-minute chart rallies to retest a prior top on the 15-minute chart, and it happens to coincide right at 3:00. When I get a rally into 3:00, that's one of those salivation times. That is especially true if I can combine it with something else like a prior top. When this happens, I want to get short the moment the low of a prior 15-minute bar gets violated. When I short or go long at the 3:00 reversal time, I am looking to exit the position at the next reversal time, which is at 3:00.

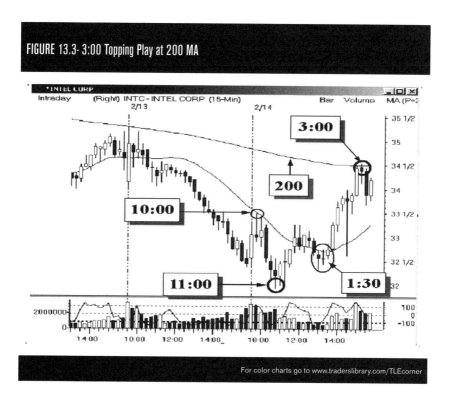

FIGURE 13.3- 3:00 Topping Play at 200 MA

For color charts go to www.traderslibrary.com/TLEcorner

In Figure 13.3, we are seeing another. This is a 15-minute chart of Intel Corp. (INTC), and it is rallying into the 3:00 reversal time. Look at how many things are combining on this play. There is, of course, the all-important 3:00 reversal time. At 3:00, the stock rallies right into the declining 200-period moving average. This is when the odds begin to increase dramatically. When you have multiple concepts coming together and the stock has already run an excessive amount into a reversal time, the odds demand that you take in that play.

> Excessive runs, reversal times, moving averages, reversal bars, and increased volume can make any intraday stock movement into a high-odds trading pattern.

The Most Powerful Strategy in the Micro Setup

Here we go with the last trading strategy. It is the potent late day breakout play. Here is what we need to have. First, we want to make sure the stock is up on the day.

Criteria two, the stock needs to be above its opening price. Note that it is possible for a stock to be up on the day and below its opening price. That is not acceptable for this trade. For this trade, the stock must be up compared to yesterday's close and above today's open.

The third criteria: The stock should be trading at or near the high of the day, basing sideways during lunch. I want to see the market

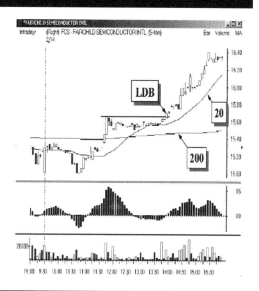

FIGURE 13.4- The Late Day Breakout (LDB)

Late Day Breakout

Criteria

1) Stock is *up* on the day

2) Stock is *above* its opening price

3) Stocks is trading at or near the *high* of the day

4) Stock breaks out *late* in the day (anytime after 2:30 EST).

For color charts go to www.traderslibrary.com/TLEcorner

makers go to lunch, and when they go to lunch I'm going to be watching the stock like a hawk. If I see a stock during lunch that does not drift down, but basically goes sideways during lunchtime when the big man's away, I know that if the first move was up, now the second move is sideways at or near the high of the day, the third move is going to be up to continue the first move.

The fourth and final criteria, the stock breaks out late in the day, after 2:30 EST.

Take a look at this 5-minute chart in Figure 13.4. I want you to note that the last move on the 5-minute chart was up, then our market makers went to lunch. Note how flat and tight the sideways pattern was. The moment after 2:30, that the stock trades to a new daily high or above the last consolidation, the microtrader is all over it, looking for a micro-explosion to the upside.

Note that the stock rallies right into, you guessed it, lunchtime. Note how the stock is basing at its high during lunchtime and is not dropping. That's a sign of strength. While it is at or near the high of the day, late in the day, after 2:30, the stock explodes to a new daily high. The microtrader is attempting to capitalize by zeroing in on the breakout.

Here are the criteria again. Criteria one, up on the day. Criteria two, the stock is above its opening price. Three, the stock is basing at or near the high of the day. This is an indication of strength. Sometime late, after 2:30 EST, the stock breaks to a new daily high. This stock has done nothing but continue the first move. This is the easiest trading pattern to make money. And you know what, it happens every single day.

By understanding the three phases of the trading day, and how stock prices revolve around the nine micro reversal times, you can effectively use the tactics I have shown you in all three phases of the trading day to consistently take money out of the market.

Self-test questions

1. The play often done at 3:00 p.m. each day is similar to what other play?

   a. The 1:30 p.m. Reversal Play.
   b. The 200-Period Moving Average Play.
   c. The 10:00 a.m. Topping and Bottoming Play.
   d. None of the above.

2. Why are plays entered during Phase Two often held until 3:00 p.m.?

   a. Because 3:00 p.m. tends to be a key afternoon reversal time.
   b. If a Phase Two trade hasn't hit your target by 3:00 p.m., it probably won't, so it's best to exit.
   c. The final hour of each market day usually offers good entry opportunities so you want to free up resources to take advantage of them.
   d. Trading activity begins to slow as market participants get ready to go home.

3. The chances of success with a trade increase greatly when multiple indicators come together, so be sure to watch:

   a. How a stock acts when approaching proven reversal times.
   b. Whether a stock is nearing a 200-period moving average.
   c. If there is any increase in trading volume associated with a reversal bar.
   d. All of the above.

4. Which of the following is NOT a criterion for a Late Day Breakout Play?

    a. The stock must be up on the day.

    b. The stock must be trading above its opening price.

    c. The stock is trading at or near its high for the day.

    d. The stock is trading at or near its 200-period moving average.

5. A good "early warning signal" for a potential Late Day Breakout Play is:

    a. The stock traded lower all morning, then reversed around lunch time.

    b. The stock rallied all morning, then traded flat during the Phase Two doldrums.

    c. The stock traded flat all morning, then moved higher in spite of the slower lunch-time trading action.

    d. The stock traded lower in the morning, approaching its 200-period moving average just after lunch.

For answers, go to www.traderslibrary.com/TLEcorner

Chapter 14
Profitable Advice

The main point I would like to make in ending this section on microtrading is that all trading should be purely technical in nature, but this especially applies to microtrading. When you understand what we are doing in trading, you will come to see how futile it is to use fundamentals. It does not matter what time frame you are trading, you will soon come to understand, if you have not already, that we are trading people, not stocks.

I do not subscribe to the use of fundamental interpretation on any time frame, but even if one did believe that fundamental data was useful in long-term time frames, that information would be worthless on an intraday basis. When stocks do make significant rallies or declines, even the most consistent stocks do not move straight up or down. In other words, if the stock is going to rally $10 next month, it does not go up 5 cents every 20 minutes in a perfect, straight line. It may rally very hard for several days and then pull back for several days. If you have a long bias toward the stock on one of the days that the stock is pulling back, you'll be a loser, even though the stock may be higher a month from now. The microtrader cares about who is winning the battle today. On some days, the long-term underdog wins the battle, and the microtrader needs to be on that side.

The microtrader needs to devoid themselves of any preconceived bias that has arisen from any kind of news event, analyst comment,

FIGURE 14.1- Delta Airlines Inc.

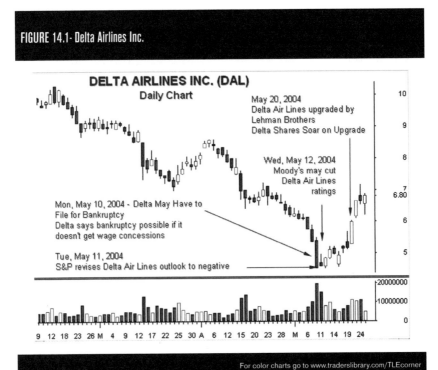

company statement, or rumor. The microtrader does not care about the actual content of the above mentioned items. What matters are people's reactions. When investing, you are relying on news and announcements and fundamental data. Look at how well timed the "bad news" is for Delta Airlines. There are many, many examples of this, as you'll see in Figure 14.1.

The concept here, as it often is, is that much of the news is already built into the stock price before the actual news is announced. How much? We never know. That is the whole problem. It is often the case that there is more bad news built into the price than the bad news is actually worth. This was the case of Delta Airlines. When actual bankruptcy is announced, it is not really new news. However, the professionals let the novice traders sell to their heart's desire when the bad news is announced, even though the stock has fallen for weeks prior to the announcement. As the sellers run dry, the professional buyers step up and take the stock on a wild ride to the upside.

> Trade charts and only the charts. As microtraders, our job is to read the reaction that other people have to any event that occurs. It is not our job to guess where the stock may go.

Measuring Reward to Risk

You have found a trade that meets the criteria that the strategy requires. What now determines if you take the trade? What if there are dozens of these trades that you can find every hour that meet the criteria, but you are only able to trade four of them, or two, or one? How do you determine the best one?

One of the things you will do is try to find the best examples of quality in the trades you take. Naturally, all trades that meet your minimum criteria are not the same. Another one of the things that you will look at to determine if you take any particular trade is the reward-to-risk presented by the trade. As I mentioned previously, the reward-to-risk, or RR, is the amount to be made from the entry to the target, as compared to the amount to be lost from the entry to the stop.

Many traders will demand the possible RR for a trade be a certain number, like 3:1 (going for a $3 target with a $1 stop) or maybe even much higher. Certainly you would not risk a dollar to make a dollar, would you? Well, perhaps you might. You see, with every good there is a bad.

There is a trade-off in the RR you pick. Very simply, while the high RR trades sound best, and often are, they have the lowest odds of being obtained. So while going for 3:1 sounds better than 1:1, if you only get the 3:1 trade right one in four times, you are losing money. If you get the 1:1 trade right two out of three times, you are making money. Naturally, the 1:1 trade will be easier to achieve. So you need to analyze every trade based on the RR presented, and the likelihood that you will consistently achieve that RR. Knowing the likelihood of achieving can best be determined by tracking your results on a trade over a period of time to see how successful you are.

FIGURE 14.2- Ceradyne Daily

CERADYNE INC. (CRDN)
Daily Chart

Multiple days
Down and WRB

Gaps up
To 34.45

20ma

Let's take a look at a sample trade. Figure 14.2 is a daily chart of CRDN, and Figure 14.3 is the intraday 5-minute chart for the last day on the daily chart. On the last day on the chart, CRDN gapped up to form a tactic called a Bullish Gap Surprise, a guerrilla tactic explained in the previous section.

The play is set up properly and would call for an entry either immediately or over the 5-minute high, with a stop under yesterday's low. This is the recommended entry and stop for the guerrilla play. The recommended management of this play sets up certain odds for the play. The management of the guerrilla play calls for a one-

FIGURE 14.3- Ceradyne 5-min

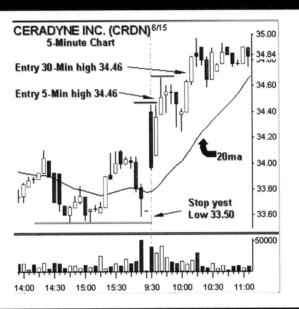

For color charts go to www.traderslibrary.com/TLEcorner

to two-day hold and may be desired if it is going to be entered or managed while the trader is away at work. Sometimes intraday traders find alternate methods of entering and managing the trade. Let's take a look at one of these.

Whenever you alter from what is recommended, the odds start changing. However, sometimes if managed properly, the outcome can be more profitable. Let's examine the odds of changing the stop from yesterday's low to today's low (today's low is 33.95). We will use the 5-minute high for entry. Study the table in Figure 14.4.

FIGURE 14.4- Scenario 1-2

Scenerio 1, By the Book, Yest LOD stop

5 minute high	$34.46
Stop under yesterdays low	$33.50
Target same for all....36.00	$36.00
Risk	$0.96
Reward	$1.54
Risk $$ sample	$500.00
Share size	521
Loss if stopped	$500.00
Profit if taarget	$802.08

Scenerio 2 By the Book, Today LOD stop

5 minute high	$34.46
Stop under todays low	$33.95
Target same for all....36.00	$36.00
Risk	$0.51
Reward	$1.54
Risk $$ sample	$500.00
Share size	980
Loss if stopped	$500.00
Profit if taarget	$1,509.80

In all of these scenarios, we will keep the target the same. The goal here is to compare entries and RR options. Notice that for every successful trade, the option using today's low-of-day stop makes almost twice as much money. This is based on share sizing so that all trades have the same risked dollars. (If you use a constant share size, then the loss would be almost half, so the same concept applies). What this is saying is that while the odds of this trade stopping out are more likely using the tighter stop, it could stop out almost twice as much and still be the same money made. So the question for you to answer is: Do your trades hold the stop at least half as much using the tight stop? If yes, then it is the better option.

FIGURE 14.5- Scenario 3

Scenerio 3, 30 minute high, Yest LOD stop

30 minute high	$34.66
Stop under yesterdays low	$33.50
Target same for all....36.00	$36.00
Risk	$1.16
Reward	$1.34
Risk $$ sample	$500.00
Share size	431
Loss if stopped	$500.00
Profit if taarget	$577.59

Let's look at changing the entry criteria. A trader may say that waiting for the 30-minute high will give the trade higher odds of success. While possibly true, the RR could change so much at the 30-minute high that it may not make sense. Look at the numbers in Figure 14.5.

In this case, the 30-minute high is not that far away, so the profit does not change much. It is lower, and the question is, will this entry produce enough success to make up for the lower dollars made every time?

FIGURE 14.6- Ceradyne Intraday

Intraday (Right) CRDN - Ceradyne, Inc. (1-Min) Bar Volume MA (P=20) MA (P=10)
6/15

Pullback into 9:35 reversal time using a one-minute chart

Entry 34.08
Stop 33.95

For color charts go to www.traderslibrary.com/TLEcorner

FIGURE 14.7- Scenrio 4

Scenerio 4 PBS on pullback, Yest LOD Stop

PBS entry	$34.08
Stop under yesterdays low	$33.50
Target same for all....36.00	$36.00
Risk	$0.58
Reward	$1.92
Risk $$ sample	$500.00
Share size	862
Loss if stopped	$500.00
Profit if taarget	$1,655.17

Scenerio 4 PBS on pullback, 1-min PBS Stop

PBS entry	$34.08
Stop under 1-minute PBS	$33.95
Target same for all....36.00	$36.00
Risk	$0.13
Reward	$1.92
Risk $$ sample	$500.00
Share size	3846
Loss if stopped	$500.00
Profit if taarget	$7,384.62

For color charts go to www.traderslibrary.com/TLEcorner

Now, let's take a look at entries by combining this tactic with another tactic. Let's buy the Pristine Buy Setup on the pullback to support at reversal time—a true microtrader's entry. The entry tactic is shown in Figure 14.6.

CRDN pulls back to support during the very first reversal time, 9:35 EST. This requires a 1-minute chart to be used. The entry is over the high of that lowest 1-minute bar, and a stop could revert back to yesterday's low, or, for the true 1-minute Pristine Buy Setup, under the low of the same bar. This reduces the risk tremendously. Let's look at the numbers in Figure 14.7 using this last option.

Using the prior day's low reduces this profit to about the same as using the 5-minute high with today's low-of-day stop. This is just a coincidence. Taking the 1-minute Pristine Buy Setup with that earlier entry keeps the RR the same even though you are now using yesterday's stop. The drawback is that using this entry is no guarantee that the stock will continue to move up. Many more will stop out.

Last is the ultimate in RR—using the 1-minute entry and stop. This now creates 4 to 12 times the profit when the target is hit. The analysis must now be made: Can the target be achieved often enough under these tight entry and stop criteria to produce more dollars on a regular basis? Again, tracking of your plays under different options will help you do this analysis for any tactic you choose to study.

Conclusion

The microtrading style makes up an essential part of the full-time trader's arsenal. You can enjoy most of the strategies found in other time frames, but play them at an accelerated pace. By using a variety of small time frame charts and strategies, there are a multitude of opportunities every trading day. I hope you have enjoyed learning some of my favorite tactics for today's microtrader.

Self-test questions

1. More than any other form of trading, microtrading should be purely technical in nature because:

   a. The short time frame makes looking at fundamentals useless.
   b. Only with charts can you recognize key entry and exit points.
   c. Microtrading is more about trading people – i.e., emotions – than about trading stocks.
   d. All of the above.

2. If three stocks meet the minimum criteria for a microtrade, but you only have enough cash available to do one, which one should you choose?

   a. The one with the lowest stock price.
   b. The one with the highest potential reward.
   c. The one with the best quality – i.e., the most indicators supporting the signal.
   d. The one with the steepest trendline in the direction you want to trade.

3. The second leading determinant for deciding among trades that meet your minimum criteria is a strong reward-to-risk ratio, but there is one drawback. What is it?

    a. Trades with high RR ratios are much harder to find.
    b. Too many other traders will be trying to take the same position.
    c. Trades with higher RR ratios have a lower probability of success.
    d. Positions with high RR ratios are less exciting to trade.

4. Positioning a stop under today's low rather than under yesterday's low will do what?

    a. Lower your potential risk on a per-share basis.
    b. Reduce the likelihood that you will be stopped out before hitting your target.
    c. Lower your potential reward-to-risk ratio.
    d. Force you to trade a smaller number of shares to stay within your dollar risk limit.

5. The key question to ask when setting targets and stops as criteria for microtrades is what?

   a. Will the resulting RR ratio be high enough to satisfy me.
   b. Are the targets and stops consistent with the 20- and 200-day moving averages.
   c. Can the target be achieved often enough to produce more dollars of profit on a regular basis.
   d. Can I deal with the emotional stress of targets and stops of this magnitude.

For answers, go to www.traderslibrary.com/TLEcorner

PART 3

Core Trading

Chapter 15
What is Core Trading?

Core trading is a style of market play that typically covers a holding period of several weeks to several months. There are two forms of core trading: the macro style and the micro style.

Core trading today has become the new style of investing. People are very aware that holding stocks on the buy-and-hold theory doesn't work anymore. The core trader uses weekly charts to make entries and exits. Core trading is often used on key stocks and indexes, especially the indexes or items that mimic the entire market, or major chunks of the market. Some examples of these are the "Qs" (the QQQQ, which is the symbol for the NASDAQ 100 tracking stock); the SPYDERS (the SPY, which is the symbol for the S&P-500 tracking stock); or the Diamonds (the DIA, which is the symbol for the Dow Industrials tracking stock.)

FIGURE 15.1- Pristine Core Trading vs. Investing

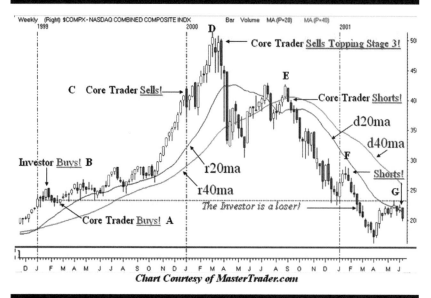

Weekly (Right) $COMPX- NASDAQ COMBINED COMPOSITE INDX   Bar Volume MA (P*20)   MA (P*40)

Chart Courtesy of MasterTrader.com

For color charts go to www.traderslibrary.com/TLEcorner

Let's take a look at how the investor compares to the core trader. Figure 15.1 is a weekly chart of the NASDAQ composite index. It is in Japanese candlestick form and it has a 20-period moving average and a 40-period moving average. The only reason color-coded volume is not shown is because this is the actual NASDAQ index and it does not have volume information.

I want you to note on the left side of the chart the 20-period moving average and 40-period moving average are rising. On the right side of the chart, the 20-period moving average and 40-period moving average are pointing down. This is a very simple, basic, visual observation. This chart covers 1999, 2000, and half of 2001. Each bar represents five trading days.

Let's assume the core trader trained by Pristine buys near the rising 20-moving average at point A. The successful, trained core trader never buys any stock unless it is near the 20-period moving average.

Let's also assume the investor buys at point B. The typical investor will tend to buy after a stock rallies. Why? Because almost every single typical investor feels the stock must first prove that it is worthy of their money. The typical investor says, "Show me that you deserve my money, stock, and then I will give you my money." So the stock rises and rises and says, "Have I shown you yet?" "Yes, you've shown me. Time to buy."

This is the first difference. The trained core trader says, "I will only buy after a period of pain, after three, four, five black bars in a row that have pulled back toward the 20-period moving average."

Let's look at how they both manage. The investor, of course, is on buy-and-hold mode. So he or she is hanging on. The core trader looks to sell at C and, if any left, or if he re-enters, again at D. The investor is in Nirvana having bought in early 1999 and continuing to hold throughout this entire rally.

We now have, on the right side of the chart, a declining 20-period moving average and a declining 40-period moving average. The 20-period moving average is below the 40-period moving average, and both moving averages are pointing the way downward. The core trader who follows the trend, now that we are in a downtrend, would short the market at E, F, and again at G. These are all sell setups I will be showing you.

The investor, who was in Nirvana, suddenly finds, two years later, that he or she is an absolute loser in the market. Some of you may be saying that you would never hold through that decline. The truth is the vast majority did. Perhaps you were one of them.

Core trading is the key to capturing substantially larger gains than your typical swing trader and microtrader can expect to achieve. I believe it is a very important part of every trader's trading arsenal or trading program. It is the part that should be applied, in my opinion, to your IRAs and KEOUGH plans, your children's trust funds, and any part of your portfolio that you do not designate to produce income.

Self-test questions

1. Core trading is a style best suited to traders with what time frame?

   a. Ultra short-term – i.e., intraday.
   b. One to two days.
   c. Three days to a week.
   d. Several weeks to several months.

2. Core traders tend to focus on what?

   a. Stocks of lower-priced issues with high volatility.
   b. Stable stocks paying relatively high dividends.
   c. Blue Chip stocks or indexes that mimic the entire market.
   d. ETFs that track specialty indexes for specific industry groups.

3. The successful, trained core trader never buys any stock or index unless it is where?

   a. Above a rising trendline connecting past lows.
   b. Below its 200-period moving average.
   c. At or near its 20-period moving average.
   d. Above its high for the previous five trading periods.

4. The trained core trader tells the market what?

    a. "I will only buy when you have shown me prolonged strength."

    b. "I will only buy after a period of pain."

    c. "I will only buy once you've begun an upward reversal."

    d. "I will only buy after the Fed cuts interest rates."

5. Core trading can be described as what?

    a. A trading program offering substantially larger gains than swing trading or microtrading.

    b. A more conservative trading approach suitable for use in IRAs and KEOGH plans.

    c. A longer-term trading program more appropriate for investors who can't watch the markets every minute of every day.

    d. All of the above.

For answers, go to www.traderslibrary.com/TLEcorner

Chapter 16

Micro versus Macro Styles

A micro core play has the trader entering off of a weekly chart in the same area a macro trade would be entered, but the micro core trader doesn't like to experience even temporary pain. So, the micro core trader looks to sell after a series of white bars, before a black bar develops when a target is hit; when a black bar forms, closing under a prior bar; or a combination of these two. There are targets when the stock would be sold and a tight management policy keeps the trader from losing profits along the way. Usually that is done with a trailing stop using a bar-by-bar approach. The theory in general is: Any sign of weakness would be your key to get out.

The macro trader doesn't care about these smaller setbacks. He or she will look to sell on the first major black bar, far away from the 20-period moving average, or when the weekly uptrend breaks. A macro approach would have the goal of staying with the play as long as the uptrend remains in place. On a core trade, that would mean staying with the position as long as the weekly chart is in an uptrend. This could keep you in the play a long time.

When using this method, the exit strategy must be clearly defined. Typically that means we maintain higher highs and lows based on pivots, or that we remain mostly above the rising 20-period moving average, or a combination of the two. The macro core trader looks to ride the entire macro move and ignores the miniature, temporary, weekly setbacks. I am not talking about strategies yet. I'm just talking about basic concepts just to get your thinking on the right page. We'll get to specific tactics and techniques later.

Another sell signal for the macro core trader is when a black bar develops far from the 20-period moving average. Remember to always watch the 20-period moving average. When the stock pulls back toward a rising 20-period moving average, I step in to buy. If it rallies way away from the 20-period moving average, then forms a black bar, I sell.

As a microtrader, I don't care where the stock is when I sell. I buy near the 20-period moving average, but after three to five white bars, I'm out. I may miss out on a few weeks to the upside, but I don't mind. I'm looking for smaller, bite-size core trading profits and taking the meat out of every move.

Here is how the difference looks on a real chart managed both ways. Figures 16.1 and 16.2 are the same weekly chart. They are

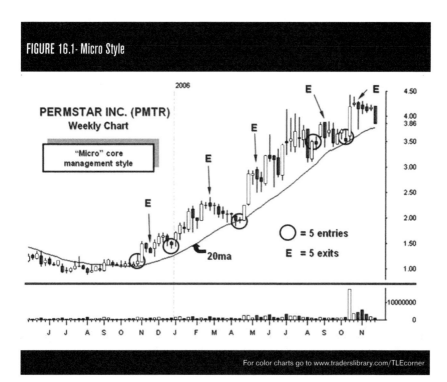

FIGURE 16.1- Micro Style

PERMSTAR INC. (PMTR)
Weekly Chart

"Micro" core
management style

20ma

◯ = 5 entries

E = 5 exits

For color charts go to www.traderslibrary.com/TLEcorner

just marked differently to show how the trade would be managed in a micro versus macro style.

Figure 16.1 shows the micro style of management. After every entry, the stock is managed until it hits a target, and/or until its trail stops on a bar-by-bar trail stop that begins after the second day. A bar-by-bar trail stop means that you would set your stop every day to the prior bar's low, plus a 5- to 20-cent cushion. This would start on the third bar. The first two bars use the original stop. Since every entry has an exit, re-entries are possible on weekly Pristine Buy Setups or Breakouts. This chart had quite a few setups, allow-

Micro versus Macro Styles | 233

ing for re-entry several times. All of the entries are marked with circles, the exits with the letter E. You would have been in and out five times over the year. Note that all the entries are near the rising 20-period moving average. I will be showing you some of these tactics soon.

The downside is that the micro style requires more management, more commissions, and most important, possible lost opportunity. This was a very friendly chart because it always had another entry. The problem is, sometimes the stock just keeps going, and there is no re-entry. So this style may have you sitting empty. The advantage

FIGURE 16.2- Macro Style

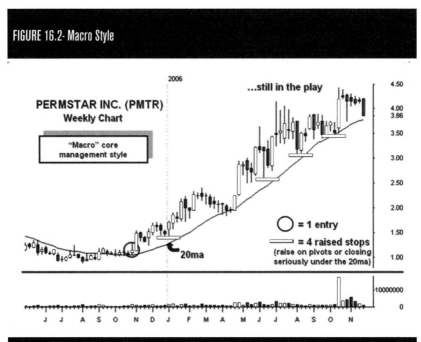

is, you never sit through a pullback, and had the uptrend broke, you would have been out with more profit than the macro method.

Figure 16.2 shows the macro style of management. There was only one entry. The stock was managed by raising stops whenever a new pivot formed. On this chart, that management kept you in the entire time. You would have had one entry, and would have still been in this play with your stop under the October pivot (white line). Note that I mentioned there is a second way to exit the macro style. That is when a white bar forms far away from the rising 20-period moving average. On this chart, that never really happened. There were times the stock got pretty far above the moving average, but most never closed black. You may have opted to exit a couple of these that were marginally far from the moving average. If you did, you always could re-enter on the next buy setup.

The downside of the macro style of managing is that you sit through all the pullbacks. This chart was very friendly so all pullbacks were mild, but had one stopped you out, you would have given back much more profit than the micro method. The advantage is that it requires little management and so far, only one commission. Also, had the stock ever had a really strong rally, you would be in the play. In the micro style, you may have exited without a re-entry.

Some traders use a combination of techniques. They start the trade with a macro style, and as the stock becomes further and further from the 20-period moving average, they switch more to a micro management style.

The QQQQ is a unit that trades on the NASDAQ Stock Exchange. It is a tracking stock that mimics the NASDAQ 100. It is a very important item that gives us the ability to trade the entire NASDAQ 100 with one stock. I believe that core trading should primarily be applied to the entire market. Do you realize that 85% of professional money managers cannot outperform the "Spyders"; or the Qs (symbol QQQQ)?

> It is actually quite simple to outperform 85% of the money managers on Wall Street.

Eighty-five percent of professional money managers who want you to give your money to them can't outperform the market itself. Do you realize that if you simply put all of your money in the Spyders you can say that you are in the top 15% of all professional money managers? Add a little bit of timing to that and you can really outperform the market and 85% of those money managers.

Self-test questions

1. A micro core player will generally enter off the same weekly chart as a macro core trader, but will exit when?

    a. As soon as an entry opportunity for a new play is spotted.
    b. After a series of white bars, when a target is hit before a black bar develops.
    c. As soon as the stock price approaches its 200-period moving average.
    d. When a combination of A and B is observed.

2. The macro trader has a different perspective, ignoring small moves and holding a long position until which of the following occurs?

    a. A major black bar forms very near the 200-period moving average.
    b. Three consecutive black bars form on the daily chart.
    c. The uptrend breaks on the weekly chart.
    d. The 20-period moving average flattens out.

3. Micro core traders closely manage their stops, resetting them when and where?

    a. Hourly at a level 5 to 10 cents below the current price level.
    b. Daily at a level 5 to 20 cents below the prior bar's low.
    c. Daily at a level 20 to 25 cents below the prior day's close.
    d. Weekly at a level 25 to 50 cents below the prior week's high.

4. The micro style of core trading has several disadvantages, including what?

    a. You have to spend more time watching the market and managing your trades.

    b. Commissions are higher and tax consequences are greater.

    c. The early exit strategy can result in significant opportunity loss.

    d. All of the above.

5. In managing a position, macro style traders raise their stops:

    a. Daily, so long as a series of white bars continues.

    b. Whenever a new pivot forms.

    c. Whenever the stock moves farther above the 20-period moving average.

    d. Whenever you feel like locking in more of your profits.

For answers, go to www.traderslibrary.com/TLEcorner

Chapter 17

Tools of the Core Trader

So far, I have just been talking in generalities. Now, let's take a look at the tools of the core trade. We're going to zero in on virtually every single tactic or technique that would have put you in the right buys and the right sells on that NASDAQ chart I reviewed. The charting tools are simple, and the first two are the same that we've used for our guerrilla and micro tactics. Let's review.

First, we want weekly charts displayed in Japanese candlestick form.

Second, we want color-coded volume at the bottom of the chart (Figure 17.1). Your charting package should allow you to add color-coding to your volume and to place the volume bars where you like. Most packages allow for this.

FIGURE 17.1- Weekly Chart with Volume

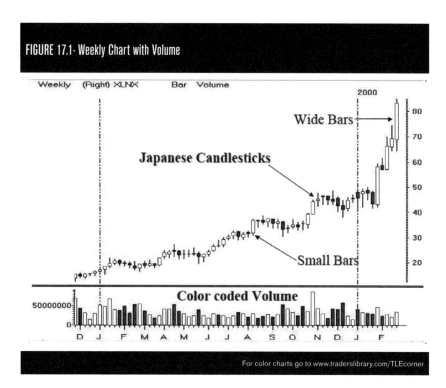

The understanding of volume, in conjunction with price, is critical to your success as a trader. Traders who understand these two can make a living in the markets without the need of anything else. Now, despite what I just said, the concept of volume is often misunderstood and overused. There are entire books written on volume, but when it comes down to it, volume really serves two main purposes. Increases in volume can help identify the beginning of new moves and they can help identify the ending of old moves. We'll discuss more on volume later.

> Traders who understand price and volume can make a living in the markets.

The 20- and the 40-Period Moving Averages

Next we want to display the 20-period moving average and the 40-period moving average. These two are your buddy system. All of my moving averages are simple, as I have found that nothing else works better. I use 20- and 40-period simple moving averages on all weekly and daily charts. The 20-period simple moving average is a staple that should be on all of your charts.

FIGURE 17.2- Core Trading Tools

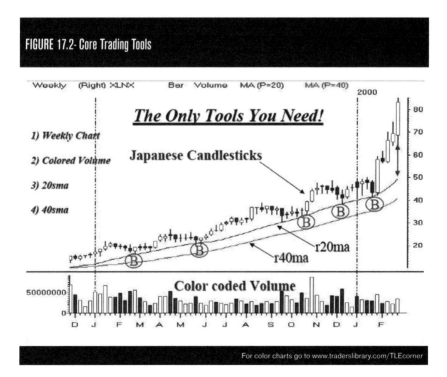

> Simple moving averages are used because nothing has proved to work better.

Let's take a look at the weekly chart in Figure 17.2 as an example. It is a weekly chart with Japanese candlesticks and at the bottom we have color-coded volume. The simple 20-period moving average is in place, as is the simple 40-period moving average.

I want you to note something interesting about this chart. We're looking at the entire year of 1999 and the beginning of year 2000. Look at the size of the bars during '99. They are small. Now look at the size of the bars in the beginning of 2000. This is a very subtle sign that the stock is in the last stretch and diving for the finish line. It takes a lot of ammunition to produce bars like this, but the ammunition in the market is not limitless. It is like a machine gun. If you shoot a machine gun slowly, the bullets will last a longer period of time, producing small bars. But press on the lever and speed up the bullets to produce big bars and you're going to run out of ammunition. Can you see how far away from the 20-period moving average this is and can you imagine how many people still bought?

I want you to also note something interesting in Figure 17.2. For an entire year, the 20-period moving average served as a major floor support under the stock. Successful core traders buy pullbacks toward the 20-period moving average and sell on multiple white bars away from the 20-period moving average. They buy near the 20 and sell away from the 20. Again, if there's one thing I can convey to you with clear understanding, let it be this.

> Keep it simple. You will have plenty of help making things complicated if you want it, but the best traders keep it simple.

You are to never, ever, touch another stock in your entire trading career if it is way away from the 20-period moving average. I would even add that you should never think about buying a stock unless it is after a multiple series of black bars to the downside. Step in, you buy after pain and you sell greed. Most traders have it reversed. They buy greed and sell after three to five black bars. That's backwards. All they need to do is flip that around.

> You are to never, ever, touch another stock in your entire trading career if it is way away from the 20-period moving average.

The weekly chart, color-coded volume, 20-period moving average, 40-period moving average—those are all you need. Everything else you add is superfluous. It doesn't mean it is useless, it just means that it's giving you the same information, just differently. I keep it simple and go straight to the horse's mouth. In trading, that means price and volume. That includes two major moving averages, which have a very specific purpose, and then basic concepts like three to five black bars down, three to five white bars up, close to the 20-period moving average, and far away from the 20-period moving average. You will be in that top 7% with basic concepts like that.

One Warning: Do Not Overindulge

How can it be made complicated? One way is by overusing technical indicators. These are various studies you can superimpose on your charts that will allegedly help you determine proper buy and sell points. There are charting packages available today that contain hundreds of technical indicators. Just the simple fact that there are hundreds available should tell you the value of any one of them.

They are often very popular with novice traders because they tend to represent something newcomers to the market like to see. Many new traders are often searching for the Holy Grail of trading. They're looking for that one market guru or that one indicator that will deliver consistent profits time and time again. Something you need to understand about technical indicators is that they all have one thing in common: they are all taking the past price and volume data on your charts and creating a new line from old data.

> All technical indicators have one thing in common: They use the existing price and volume data to create a new line to put on the chart. It is never new information.

They have a value in many instances, but should never be used to make buy and sell decisions. Traders often find one particular indicator that works on a certain stock for a certain period of time and feel they have found the Holy Grail to trading. However, they soon discover that the indicator needs to be tweaked and adjusted and eventually discarded. For making buy and sell decisions, there is nothing superior to the price pattern itself.

The danger is in feeling that any single indicator will give you consistent profits. I have seen traders use so many indicators on their charts it is difficult to even see the price bars through the mess of spaghetti on their chart. Some traders find that one or two particular indicators help them in the process of making a decision, and that is perfectly fine.

Moving averages are actually technical indicators. While they are the simplest of the indicators, they do present us with valuable information. But I do not use a moving average to determine my entry, only the general area. I use moving averages as a guide to help determine the quality of the trend. The proper use of technical indicators is to use them as a filter. By that I mean, once your decision is made to enter a position, you may choose not to because the indicator has not "approved" the trade.

> Technical indicators should not be the basis for buy and sell decisions.

The Battle between Buyer and Seller

Now, here is where we start getting into the core concepts that form the entire trading philosophy. Every single bar, every single week, is nothing more than a battle between two groups: the buyers and sellers. If you are looking at a chart, every bar was a battle. You must develop the skill of determining who won the battle.

> You must learn how to determine who is winning the individual battles because you had better be betting on the side that is winning the war.

Of course, we know that every bar has four prices: an open, the low, the close, and the high. Now, when the closing price is above the opening price, the buyers won. Remember, every bar is one battle in a never-ending war. Successful trading will depend on one thing, your ability to determine who was winning the war at this particular time. Do you know why? You had better be betting with the side that's winning the war. If the stock closes above its opening price, the buyers won that battle. If the stock closes below its opening price, the sellers won that individual battle. This is an important concept. It's very basic and it's very simple. Do not let the simplicity fool you because this is going to form the entire foundation for a very phenomenal trading methodology.

Now, here's a very important statistical fact. Bulls and bears, or buyers and sellers, cannot consistently win more than five battles in a row. Each side will typically give up the power to the other side after three to five battles. Three white bars in a row, the sellers are close to grabbing control. Three black bars in a row and the buyers are close to taking control. It is that simple, but it is powerful.

This one concept alone, if you get it right, will help you become a very accurate stock price predictor. Statistically, one color cannot last more than five in a row without trouble, whether it's five black in a row or five white in a row.

Now this next statement is key: If the bulls or bears win significantly more than five bars in a row, a catastrophic loss is the price to be paid because a statistical aberration has occurred. Go far beyond five white bars in a row, and I promise you the drop to the downside will be huge. More than five black bars in a row to the downside, when the snap back happens, it will be a violent snap back to the upside.

> Fear and greed make it difficult for moves to continue more than three to five bars in either direction, and this applies on any time frame.

We are talking about weekly charts because this section is on core trading, but the concepts I'm talking to you about can be applied to any time frame. Why? Because they are the concepts of two emotions, right? Fear and greed. Fear and greed exist in all time frames, so it will always apply.

Self-test questions

1. Core traders need Japanese candlestick charts that show what as well as bars?

    a. Red and green moving average lines.
    b. Color-coded trendlines.
    c. Color-coded volume indicators.
    d. Red and green Stochastic indicators.

2. Increases in volume can sometimes indicate what?

    a. Greater market awareness of a stock?
    b. Growing overall interest in stock investing in general.
    c. A new move is beginning or an old move is ending.
    d. The company has made a new public offering of stock.

3. The charts used by core traders should also include what two moving averages?

    a. The 10- and 20-period moving averages.
    b. The 20- and 40-period moving averages.
    c. The 20- and 200-period moving averages.
    d. The 40- and 200-period moving averages.

4. Successful core traders follow what proven trading tactic?

    a. Buy low and sell high.

    b. Buy after pain and sell when you see greed.

    c. Buy after three white bars and sell after three black bars.

    d. Buy when the stock is far away from its 20-period moving average and sell when it gets close to it again.

5. Statistical research of the markets has shown that, in the daily battle between bulls and bears:

    a. Bulls win more short-term battles, creating longer upward trends.

    b. Bears react with greater ferocity, pushing prices down faster than they went up.

    c. Neither bulls nor bears can consistently win more than five battles in a row.

    d. The stronger an initial bullish or bearish move, the weaker the subsequent correction.

For answers, go to www.traderslibrary.com/TLEcorner

Chapter 18
The Key Events

It is now time to take the information I have shown you and look for the actual plays on the weekly chart. In this section, we are going to be looking for the setups that form the strategies we will be playing as core traders.

Figure 18.1 shows the pictures of greed. Here are three white bars. What are you thinking of doing? Selling. Now with four white bars. You're rubbing your hands together doing what? You should still be thinking, "Sell." With five white bars in a row, you should really be thinking "Sell." Do you realize that most individual market players buy after five bars up? Do you realize that the No. 1 rule from the analysts is to buy new highs when 75% of all new highs fail? In virtually every single analyst book, you will hear them cry to buy new highs. Why do you think that's so? Because when major

FIGURE 18.1- 3 to 5 Bar Rallies/ Pictures of Greed

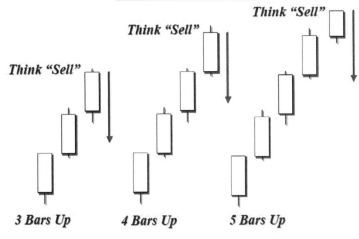

Pictures of Greed

Think "Sell"

Think "Sell"

Think "Sell"

3 Bars Up   4 Bars Up   5 Bars Up

sellers have to sell and want to sell, they need buyers. This is the way Wall Street operates. You should be smart about this. So, three to five bars up, you're thinking, "Sell." Too much greed has already happened. You want to be playing on the side where big money will actually be, selling into the demand created by those buying the new high.

Here's a three- to five-bar concept to the downside as seen in Figure 18.2. With three black bars, what are you thinking, buying or selling? Think "Buy," but don't actually buy because you see three black bars. Just think buy. We'll get to that. With four black bars, it's party time.

FIGURE 18.2- 3 to 5 Bar Rallies/ Pictures of Pain

Pictures of Pain

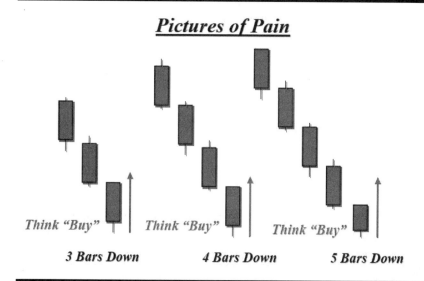

Think *"Buy"*   Think *"Buy"*   Think *"Buy"*

3 Bars Down   **4 Bars Down**   **5 Bars Down**

For color charts go to www.traderslibrary.com/TLEcorner

I have a 7-year-old daughter whose name is Rebecca. Every week, we sit down and we have a little lesson on the market. She thinks Daddy plays computer games for a living and she likes it. Every week during our lesson, here is one of the things I teach her. I say, "OK, sweetheart, how many bars do you see?." "Ten", she says. "OK, how many of the 10 bars are white?" "Seven," she says. "How many are black?" "Three." "Who is in control, sweetheart?" "The buyers, Daddy!" That's simple, right? "OK, how many bars do you see now, sweetheart?" "Twenty." "How many black bars?" "Fourteen black bars out of the 20." "How many white bars?" "Six." "Who is in control, sweetheart?" "The sellers!" This is a simple concept. Simply counting bars.

> The public is told to buy new highs, but the pros are selling at those new highs.

If black bars mean the sellers won the battle and white bars mean the buyers won that battle, if I count the number of bars in my chart, whichever one comes up with more winning battles is winning the war. That's the side that I should be on. I know what the Bible says, right? David beat Goliath. Trust me, in trading, Goliath always wins. How do you find Goliath? You count the bars.

Figure 18.3 is a weekly chart of Intuit, a relatively popular NASDAQ stock. You can see that this stock was primarily in a sideways

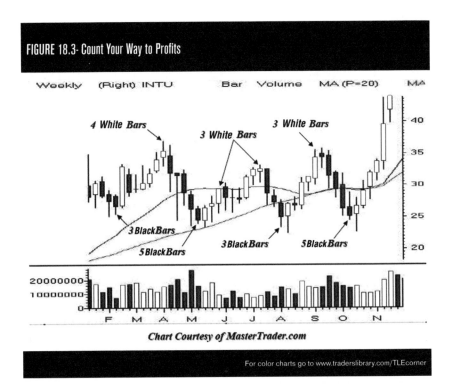

FIGURE 18.3- Count Your Way to Profits

Chart Courtesy of MasterTrader.com

trend over a period of time. I want you to look at this, starting on the left side of the chart. How many black bars? There are three. Then it pulls back toward the 20-period moving average.

Then comes how many white bars? There are four white bars in a row. Are you thinking about buying or selling? You should be thinking of selling. How many black bars? There are five and it's party time. With three white bars—stall. It doesn't mean it has to fall, but you certainly get a stall. How many white bars in a row? Three forms the top.

Look further and you see three black bars and we've got some bottoming tails there, which we'll talk about very soon. Remember, it must be three to five in a row. One, two, three, four, five— party time.

> Go through charts on your own and look for the items discussed in this book; you will be amazed how often these things occur in the market.

These are huge moves on a weekly chart. Each bar is a week, so on this move you can count six weeks and look how far away from the 20-period moving average area you are. You are thinking about doing what? Selling, right? Never again, for the rest of your life, will you ever buy a stock away from the 20-period moving average. If you get a call from your broker at 7:00 at night bothering you at dinner and he wants you to buy a stock that's way away from the 20-period moving average, your first action the next day should be to fire the broker.

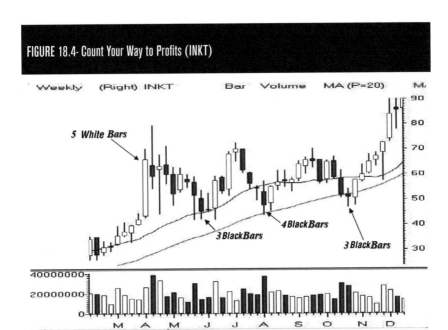

Let's count our way to profit again. Follow on Figure 18.4, beginning on the left. Five white bars in a row, way away from the 20-period moving average. I am not an interested buyer. If I'm in the stock, I'm an interested seller.

I'm stepping in looking for someone willing to give up their stock at precisely the wrong time. I'm looking for four black bars in a row.

The next move is three black bars in a row. Then a big rally, so it is far away from the 20-period moving average; I am selling. If I'm in the stock, I'm interested in handing it off to someone who does not know what they're doing.

Let's talk about bull and bear tails. We're going to get into some really interesting things now because I'm going to add some very phenomenal things to the three- to five-bar concept.

Bottoming Tails and Topping Tails

I have written several articles on bottoming tails and topping tails. It is an extremely important event. I have some traders who make their entire living off of this one concept. The concept of finding bottoming tails and topping tails, and going the other way, is a very powerful concept.

FIGURE 18.5- Bull and Bear Tails

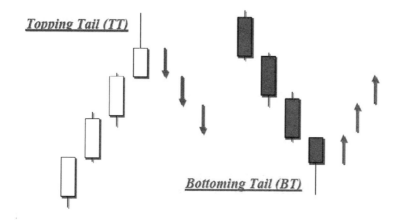

Bottoming & Topping Tails

Topping Tail (TT)

Bottoming Tail (BT)

For color charts go to www.traderslibrary.com/TLEcorner

Let's take a look at Figure 18.5. Four bars up, look what happens here. This is what I call a topping tail. It is a relatively long tail, pointing to the top, after multiple white bars. To qualify as a topping tail, at least half the bar must be tail—half or less body.

The second very important requirement—it must follow at least three white bars. It is not a topping tail if there are not three or more white bars preceding it. A topping tail indicates where large amounts of selling have occurred. Topping tails indicate major institutional sellers trying to sell quietly, but the astute chartist recognizes their action. This stock is about to do what? It drops. We already know it is about to drop because it is four white bars in a row. But four white bars plus a topping tail? You are rubbing your hands together getting ready.

> Bottoming tails are the graffiti marks of big buyers, and they should be respected.

Look at the right side of Figure 18.5. Four black bars down, plus a bottoming tail. So I know just by virtue of having four black bars in a row that I'm ready to rally, but the bottoming tail tells me I'm ready to rally right now. Multiple black bars in a row, bottoming tail, rally. Multiple white bars in a row, topping tail, time to fall.

Figure 18.6 shows the topping tails in action. This is a weekly chart of Qlogic Corp. (QLGC.) Of course, our basic items are on the chart. We have candlestick price bars, a 20-period moving average, a 40-period moving average, and volume. Notice the three black bars pull back to the rising 20-period moving average inside the

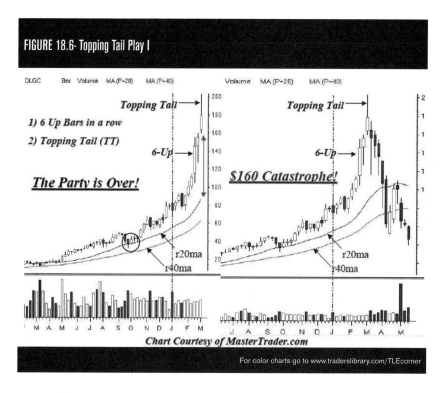

circle. That is when you, as a core trader, step up to the plate and look for someone who is willing to unload their stock after three weeks of pain they can no longer stand. The first week they had a headache, the second week they had a migraine, the third week they were crying on the shoulder of their spouse. You take the stock at the 20-period moving average and you ride the wave.

Notice that at the end of the rally, we then have six white bars in a row. Not five but six. The price is going to be big. It's going to have to be paid and the collapse is going to be enormous. Not only six bars up, but the sixth bar is capped off with a huge topping tail indicating that institutions are just dumping stock on the market.

Notice also how far away from the 20-period moving average I am. The price paid is going to be huge.

So we have six bars up in a row and a topping tail. The party is over. How much is the party over? How about a $160 catastrophe? Again, six white bars in a row, topping tail way away from the 20-period moving average, and the first black bar is going to trigger the decline.

> While bottoming tails and topping tails are excellent signs of reversal, they have to be played with a wider stop.

FIGURE 18.7- Bottoming Tail

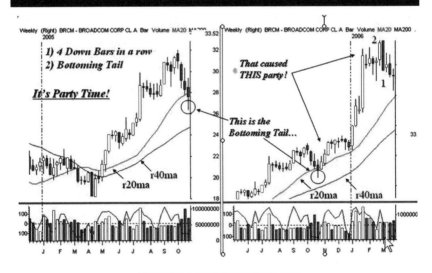

Chart Courtesy of MasterTrader.com

Let's look at the example of the bottoming tail in Figure 18.7. We have a weekly chart, rising 20-period moving average, rising 40-period moving average. When both are rising, we know that you can buy the pullbacks toward the rising 20-period moving average. We will get into how that is done shortly. Then we have four black bars in a row toward the 20-period moving average happening at the circle, on the right hand side of the chart.

This is when you step up to the plate as an interested buyer. The stock rallies, as you can see on Figure 18.7. As a micro core trader, you would have been out around the $32 area and re-entered over the $34 area. As a macro trader, you would have stayed in until the big black bar that is the fifth from the last on the right hand chart, numbered 1. Note the circles on both charts are the setup. The chart on the right is compacted because of the big rally.

Take a look at the white bar on the right hand chart that precedes the black exit bar I just mentioned. It is numbered 2. If you were not in the stock at the time, is that a good entry? A breakout to new highs? It did break out, and it did make new highs. But you should never buy that. Read above. I want you to never buy far away from the 20-period moving average.

> Professional traders always let the stock come to them. They never chase the play. This is in line with the concept of buying near the 20-period moving average and selling away from the 20-period moving average.

The Bullish and Bearish Changing of the Guard

Let's talk about the next event. This is called the Bullish and Bearish Changing of the Guard. It's a concept or name that I've given to a very frequently occurring concept in the market.

In Figure 18.8, we see four white bars in a row and look what happens? A black bar happens. This is an indication that the balance of power has shifted from the buyers to the sellers. After four white bars in a row in this example (it must be three or more), a black bar forms, which tells you that the sellers have regained control of the market. They are now in control of the war and you should be

FIGURE 18.8- Bull and Bear COG

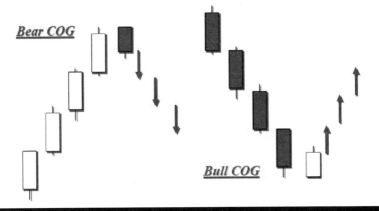

Changing of the Guard (COG)

Bear COG

Bull COG

For color charts go to www.traderslibrary.com/TLEcorner

looking for multiple black bars to follow. This is called a Bearish Changing of the Guard.

Look at the right side for the Bullish Changing of the Guard. We have four black bars followed by a white bar. This changing of the guard at the door of your money has happened. The guard at the door was a seller and he's given up and giving the controls or key to the buyers here. Now we're looking for multiple white bars to follow.

Look at some Bearish Changing of the Guard plays. Figure 18.9 is a weekly chart of Ariba Inc. (ARBA), during the heyday. I am showing you a variety of charts that include a couple of older ones.

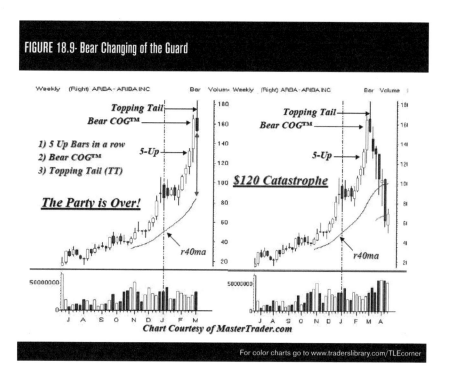

FIGURE 18.9- Bear Changing of the Guard

Chart Courtesy of MasterTrader.com

This chart and the topping tail chart of Qlogic Inc. are from the crash of 2001. I want to show you these because I want to show you how well these concepts worked during the crash that hurt so many people. If you knew then what you know now, you would have profited from the fall.

> A changing of the guard means the momentum has already shifted. If the bulls were in charge, they are tired and the bears have just taken over.

Let's check it out: five white bars in a row, not three or four, but five white bars in a row, plus a Bearish Changing of the Guard, plus a topping tail, plus way away from the 20-period moving average. Can you ask for more? These are all the ingredients coming together. You know what's about to happen, right?

A major price is going to be paid to the downside. It's going to collapse. It becomes a $120 catastrophe. Again, if there's one thing I want you to understand it's to never, ever, think about buying a stock that's way away from the 20-period moving average. And as you see, you can turn it into a profit-making opportunity. Way away from the 20-period moving average, after three to five white bars in row, a flip to a black bar, topping tail, kiss it good-bye and profit from it.

It is now time to take a look at Figure 18.10 and combine the three to five black or white bars with what we know about topping/bottoming tails and Bullish/Bearish Changing of the Guards. Start on the left with three black bars. They come in a row and the last one

FIGURE 18.10- Changing of the Guard Plays

Chart Courtesy of MasterTrader.com

has a bottoming tail. This propels the stock like a rocket. Then we have four up bars in a row plus a topping tail. What does that lead to? Five down bars in a row, of course.

Now look at this: There are five black bars in a row plus a Bullish Changing of the Guard. The guard flipped. It just went from black to white after five black in a row. That's a powerful sign. We rally three bars, and then a Bearish Changing of the Guard stalls the stock for three bars. Three more white bars and we reverse to the downside again. Next comes three down bars in a row plus a Bullish Changing of the Guard plus a bottoming tail. What more can we ask for? Three up bars in a row and another Bearish Changing of the Guard. Then five bars in a row down, a Bullish Changing of the Guard plus a bottoming tail—step on board and get ready for the ride.

These combinations happen every single day in the market and all you have to do is know the combinations and just sit and wait for them to happen. That is one of the No. 1 problems of market players: They feel they must be active at all times. But it isn't like that. You actually find several events that happen over and over again, and all you do is play the waiting game and the numbers game. You play this consistent style of trading over and over again.

Self-test questions

1. Statistically speaking, when market analysts advise investors to buy stocks making new highs, how often are they correct?

   a. 25 percent of the time.
   b. 50 percent of the time.
   c. 75 percent of the time.
   d. Only about 15 percent of market analysts are ever correct.

2. Which of the following is the strongest buy signal?

   a. Four consecutive white bars.
   b. Two consecutive black bars followed by a white 20/20 bar.
   c. Three consecutive black bars.
   d. Five consecutive black bars.

3. After three or more consecutive black bars or three or more consecutive white bars, a stock will nearly always do what?

   a. Continue in the direction of the newly established trend.
   b. Keep rising or falling until it nears its 200-day moving average.
   c. Reverse until it gets back near its 20-day moving average.
   d. You cannot tell for sure without watching more trading periods.

4. Which of the following is a very strong sell signal?

    a. Four black bars, the last one of which has a very long tail to the upside.

    b. Four white bars, the last one of which as a very long tail to the upside.

    c. Four black bars, the last one of which has very short upper and lower tails.

    d. Four white bars, the last one of which as very short upper and lower tails.

5. A Bullish Changing of the Guard occurs when you have what?

    a. Two or more consecutive white bars.

    b. A series of mixed black and white bars followed by three or more white bars.

    c. Three or more black bars followed by a white bar.

    d. Three or more white bars followed by a black bar.

For answers, go to www.traderslibrary.com/TLEcorner

Chapter 19
The Strategies

In the last chapter, we talked about setups. What makes stocks move? Three to five bars in one direction, followed by changing of the guards and bottoming tails. That is what we look for. Let's talk about where to look for these and how this will combine to make a strategy—something you can identify, find, and play over and over again. We will then talk about exactly how to play that strategy.

The Mighty 20-Period Moving Average Plays

These are what I call mighty 20-period moving average plays. I have said that if the 20-period moving average is rising, and the 40-period moving average is rising, and the 20-period moving average is above the 40-period moving average, then you can buy pull backs toward the 20-period moving average. Let's talk about that.

FIGURE 19.1- Mighty 20 MA Plays

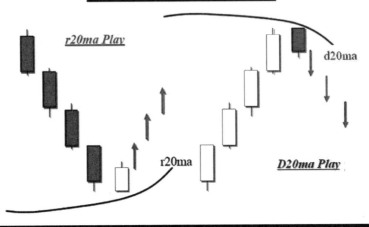

The Powerful 20ma Play

For color charts go to www.traderslibrary.com/TLEcorner

In Figure 19.1, note the first use of the moving average. It is to identify good trends. Quality trends have smooth rising moving averages and the price should respond to the 20-period moving average whenever it meets it. This is what we want to look at now. Realizing that the best trends react to the moving average, we want to use that to our advantage.

> Most traders lose because they come to the market without any real strategy. If you really press them, they cannot tell you what they are looking for that will repeat itself over and over again.

You can see the example in Figure 19.2. There are three black bars and a rising 20-period moving average. There are also three black

FIGURE 19.2- 20 MA Play I

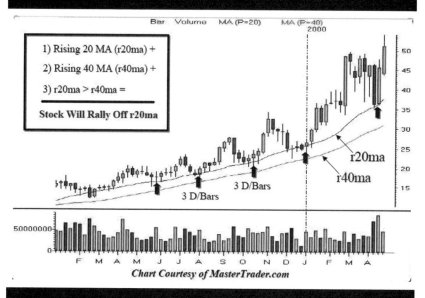

1) Rising 20 MA (r20ma) +

2) Rising 40 MA (r40ma) +

3) r20ma > r40ma =

Stock Will Rally Off r20ma

Chart Courtesy of MasterTrader.com

For color charts go to www.traderslibrary.com/TLEcorner

bars and a Bullish Changing of the Guard. You know that a multiple black bar move-back toward a rising 20-period moving average will ricochet off the 20-period moving average a high percentage of the time.

Let's take a closer look. Figure 19.2 is a weekly chart that is an excellent example of the 20-period moving average play. Each bar represents one week of trading on this chart. A rising 20-period moving average, a rising 40-period moving average, the rising 20-period moving average is above the rising 40-period moving average. I want you to note that the pullback is toward the 20-period moving average. All of this makes for a high likelihood the stock will rally off of the 20-period moving average. Note how consistently it did so.

Three to five black bars and we know the stock is ready to bounce, right? Now, if those black bars happen to end at a rising 20-period moving average, we are really talking about some nice odds. What if we happen to form a bottoming tail or a Bullish Changing of the Guard on that last bar sitting on the 20-period moving average? Well, now we are talking about a quality play, an actual strategy that you will find has high odds.

> In quality trends, prices will react to the 20-period moving average.

You should never think about buying a stock that is far away from the 20-period moving average, only one that has declined to a 20-period moving average. If you're buying, what must the 20-period moving average be doing? Rising. That increases the odds that the 20-period moving average will ricochet it back up.

The Bear Strategy

Now look at the bearish version in Figure 19.1. We have four white bars and then the declining 20-period moving average. Four white bars and a rally toward a declining 20-period moving average. The 20-period moving average should knock the stock back down, but it must be a declining moving average to do so.

FIGURE 19.3- 20 MA Play III

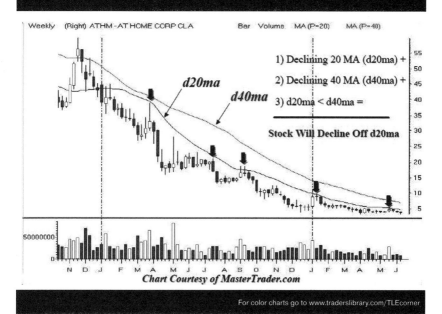

Weekly   (Right) ATHM - AT HOME CORP CL A   Bar   Volume   MA (P-20)   MA (P-40)

1) Declining 20 MA (d20ma) +
2) Declining 40 MA (d40ma) +
3) d20ma < d40ma =
_____
Stock Will Decline Off d20ma

Chart Courtesy of MasterTrader.com

For color charts go to www.traderslibrary.com/TLEcorner

If it's a declining 20-period moving average, you are going to do the reverse. Remember, it is just as easy to make money shorting to a declining 20-period moving average as it is being long into a rising 20-period moving average. Actually, it is easier. Why? Because stocks fall faster then they rally. If you don't believe that, just check out some charts over the years. Fear is stronger than greed in humans. This is a proven fact. And these are the emotions that drive stock prices. If the 20-period moving average is rising, you're a buyer. If it's declining, you're a seller on rallies to it. It seems simple, and it is, but it is very powerful.

An example of a declining 20-period moving average play is shown in Figure 19.3. Note my 20-period moving average is declining, my 40-period moving average is declining, and my 20-period moving average is below the 40-period moving average. That means that any rally toward the declining 20-period moving average should knock the stock back down.

> The more different combinations of events that come together, that are all pointing in the same direction, the higher the quality of the play.

The arrows shown are actual strategic entries. The first one is a Pristine Sell Setup. The second is a Pristine Breakdown. Remember, in a downtrend, we need a three- to five-bar rally, with maybe a topping tail or a Bearish Changing of the Guard, and as we now have learned, a declining 20-period moving average. Let's look at the Pristine Sell Setup a little bit closer (Figure 19.4).

What we need to focus on is the three- to five-bar rally. That is what we want to sell short. At a minimum, I want to see either three white bars or three higher lows (HL). That is the sign of greed that we want to sell short because it is happening into the declining 20-period moving average. It would be nice to have both, and it would also be nice to have three higher highs (HH), but that is all optional. Remember, we are in a downtrend and the white bars you are seeing are rallying back into the declining 20-period moving average.

FIGURE 19.4- Pristine Sell Setup (PSS) 20-pts.

The Setup | The Action

Main Criterion: **3 or more consecutive higher lows _or_**
3 or more _white_ bars.
Tip: Having both makes the set-up more potent.

Optional Item: **3 or more consecutive higher highs**

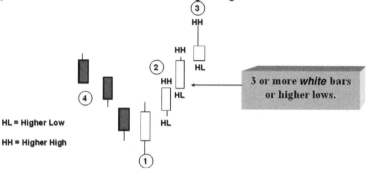

HL = Higher Low

HH = Higher High

3 or more _white_ bars or higher lows.

For color charts go to www.traderslibrary.com/TLEcorner

The Pristine Buy and Sell Setup is how you actually go long or short a stock. It provides an exact entry, and most important, an exact stop loss point. It also does not trigger unless there has been some shift in momentum, so it has very high odds.

Once we have this setup we are ready to take action. This is true the moment we have three white bars or three higher lows. We are going to take action whenever the stock trades below the low of a prior bar. If this happens after three white bars, that is fine. In this Figure, you can see that it did not trigger after three bars, so we're now on the fourth bar. If it does not trigger on the fourth bar, we

FIGURE 19.5- Pristine Short Setup (PSS)

The Setup | **The Action**

1) Short when the stock trades below the prior bar's low, _or_

2) Place a stop above the entry bar's high, or the prior bar's high, _whichever is higher_.

3) Establish the minimum target at or slightly below the prior pivot low or as discussed in the micro-macro chapter

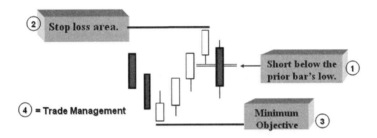

For color charts go to www.traderslibrary.com/TLEcorner

will wait until the fifth bar, and it continues that way as long as the downtrend or the declining 20-period moving average is not violated.

Now it is time for action. In Figure 19.5 you can see the stock has now traded below the prior bar. We are now going to short sell the stock if it trades below the low of the prior bar. Some traders like to give the stock an extra 5 to 20 cents before shorting, but I like to jump right in as it crosses the prior day's low.

You now know how to short in a downtrend at the declining 20-period moving average using the Pristine Sell Setup. This is what is represented by the first arrow in Figure 19.3. Notice the setup at the second arrow looks different. The stock did not really rally back to the moving average. Rather, it was so weak it simply went sideways. This is an indication that the stock is even weaker than the first setup and demands our attention even more. The setup at the first arrow happened as a result of what we call a price consolidation. Prices retraced because they were too extended. The stock falls hard, so it retraces part of the fall by a rally in price.

The second arrow represents a consolidation through time. In this case we find enough sellers to prevent the stock from even rallying a little in price and the result is a sideways action, until the existing buyers run out. This forms a sideways base that will usually resume its prior trend as it contacts the 20-period moving average.

This play, where we short a consolidation into the declining 20-period moving average, is known as a Pristine Breakdown. The action to do this is fairly simple. Your entry is below the low of the last four to six bars that make up the consolidation. Your stop will be over the high of those same four to six bars. You may sometimes opt to set the stop over the high of the bar if it is a fairly wide bar.

Once an uptrend is established, your job is to buy pullbacks (those three- to five-bar drops) and consolidation breakouts. Once a downtrend is established, your job is to short pullbacks (those three- to five-bar rallies) and consolidation breakdowns.

FIGURE 19.6- Pristine Buy Setup

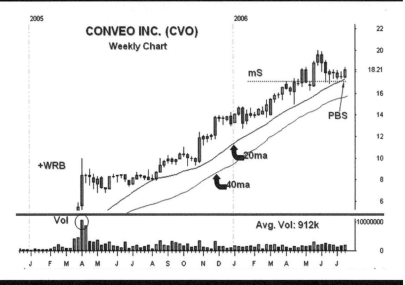

CONVEO INC. (CVO)
Weekly Chart

For color charts go to www.traderslibrary.com/TLEcorner

The Bull Strategy

Notice that these two strategies are short selling (or shorting) a stock in a downtrend into the declining 20-period moving average. As with everything in trading, this all applies exactly the same way when going long a stock that has pulled back into a rising 20-period moving average. Let's look at a quick real life example in Figure 19.6.

This is a weekly chart of Conveo Inc. (CVO). Notice that we have our setup in place. We have a rising 20-period moving average and a rising 40-period moving average. Notice how nicely the price has

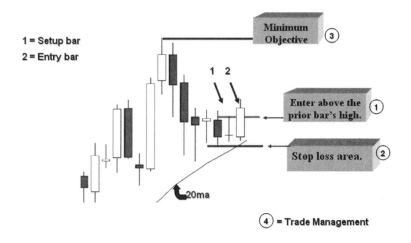

FIGURE 19.7- The PBS Up Close

1 = Setup bar
2 = Entry bar

Minimum Objective ③

1 2

Enter above the ①
prior bar's high.

Stop loss area. ②

20ma

④ = Trade Management

For color charts go to www.traderslibrary.com/TLEcorner

responded to the 20-period moving average on all pullbacks for several months. Notice that this uptrend contains a beautiful Pristine Breakout in approximately August. The setup we are looking at now is on the very right hand side of the chart. The white bar that is labeled PBS is the bar that you would be entering this play on, as it traded above the high. That prior bar is a small narrow bar known as a Doji. Let's take that area in question and make it bigger so you can see closely.

Figure 19.7 is the same stock with the entry area enlarged so you can see the four action steps at work. Bar one is known as the set up bar. Actually, the two bars prior to bar one are also setup bars, as they already came after three lower highs. However, the price never traded over one of those bars, so the setup remains intact until bar two comes along and trades over the prior high. This makes bar two the entry bar. Our protective stop loss goes under the low of bar one, and our targets and management style will depend on whether we are micro or macro core trading this position.

> While this setup is being taught as a core tactic on weekly charts, the Pristine Buy/Sell Setup can be used in all time frames.

You now know how to play a weekly Pristine Buy Setup on a three-to five-bar decline with bottoming tails or changing of the guards

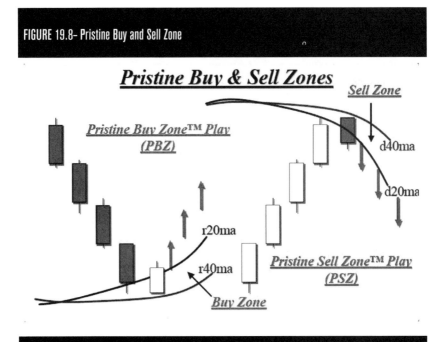

FIGURE 19.8– Pristine Buy and Sell Zone

Pristine Buy & Sell Zones

Sell Zone

Pristine Buy Zone™ Play (PBZ)

d40ma

d20ma

r20ma

r40ma

Pristine Sell Zone™ Play (PSZ)

Buy Zone

as it falls into a rising 20-period moving average. How do you find these plays? I like to keep things simple. I use Pristine ESP and the scan modules for weekly uptrends, weekly downtrends, and weekly buy/sell setups. Pristine ESP is a unique scanning tool that finds the setups I teach as well as virtually every other pattern a scanner can find. It is fast and uses very little of your computer's power. It not only saves time, but finds plays I would never find because no one can scan thousands of stocks every day.

There are other areas where this is ripe to happen besides the 20-period moving average. Let's take a look at those now.

The Pristine Buy and Sell Zone

Here is another concept called the Pristine Buy Zone and the Pristine Sell Zone. There are very few things I've actually created and this is one of them. It is not necessary to create things, it is only necessary to identify them and recognize them. Look at Figure 19.8. If we have three down bars in a row, rising 20-period moving average, rising 40-period moving average with 20-period moving average above the 40-period moving average, the space between the rising 20-period and 40-period moving average is what I call the buy zone. I realized about 12 years ago that incredible rallies occur when the stock drops between these two moving averages. That space, if they are both rising, is a phenomenal cushion and presents some very interesting buying opportunities. So if a stock drops three to five bars into the space between the rising 20-period

FIGURE 19.9- The Pristine Buy Zone

Weekly (Right) BRCM - BROADCOM CORP CL A Bar Volume MA20 MA40

1) Rising 20ma
2) Rising 40ma
3) Even space
4) Price enters PBZ

It's Rally Time!

For color charts go to www.traderslibrary.com/TLEcorner

moving average and 40-period moving average, it's a phenomenal buying opportunity.

> While the PBZ and PSZ plays can produce incredible bounces, they often are the last big move for the stock for a while.

Of course, we have the same on the reverse side. The setup would be to have multiple white bars up and a declining 20-period moving average, a declining 40-period moving average with the declining 20-period moving average below the declining 40-period moving average. If we then rally to the area between the declining 20-period moving average and 40-period moving average, that

FIGURE 19.10- The Pristine Sell Zone

space between those two moving averages is the Pristine Sell Zone. It is a phenomenal sealant, and the move to the downside should be a violent one. It sets up some incredible selling opportunities. Let's take a look at an example.

Figure 19.9 is a weekly chart of Broadcom Corp., a popular semiconductor stock. It broke out in the middle of the chart in April. That led to the pullback in October. At that point, the uptrend was under way such that we had a rising 20-period moving average and a rising 40-period moving average and a space between them that was equal or growing. You will find that sometimes the Pristine Buy Zone plays are more frequent when the rising moving aver-

The Strategies | 283

ages begin to separate a little. This pullback comes on four black bars and almost seems as if it has gone too far, but the Pristine Buy Zone springboards the stock on an incredible rally. The stock goes from around 27 to around 47 in about four months. This Pristine Buy Zone area is a very important spot.

Next is the sell zone as you see in Figure 19.10. This is a chart of the ever-so popular-Wal-Mart. We have a declining 20-period moving average, declining 40-period moving average, with the declining 20-period moving average below the declining 40-period moving average. It means that rallies are to be sold now, especially those that pull back toward the 20-period moving average, and if they

FIGURE 19.11- Climactic Buy and Sell Set Up

Climactic Buy & Sell Set-ups

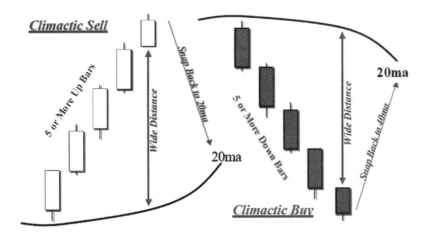

get past the 20-period moving average and enter into the zone, they are an even more phenomenal sell. How many white bars in a row? There are one, two, three white bars in a row. Then what else? A little bit of a topping tail, and right in the middle of the zone. I want you to think about the items. One is three white bars in a row. A topping tail is two. The third is the Pristine Sell Zone. These are phenomenal combinations.

The Climactic Buy and Sell Setup

I have one more strategy to discuss with you. This again is going to be based on location; that is, exactly where it is happening on the chart. You have seen the 20-period moving average play and the Pristine Buy and Sell Zone. Now we want to see what happens when we get very far extended from the 20-period moving average. It is called the Climactic Buy and Sell Setup. It is the one I want you zeroing in on. Remember, I talked to you about the fact that stocks cannot stay very far away from the 20-period moving average very long. You can make a living in the markets by just waiting for your favorite stock or the entire market, it doesn't matter: Just get way away from the 20-period moving average, and then you step in on the first color change. It's simple. That's it.

Let's take a look at Figure 19.11. I have five white bars up and now I know I'm far away from the 20-period moving average. Greed has run five races in a row. Greed is tired now and it's going to give up the ghost to fear. The 20-period moving average is like a leash—

it is going make the price get yanked back to the downside. It will snap back toward the 20-period moving average.

> The Pristine-trained trader goes with the trend 92% of the time. The only time he or she goes against the trend is the climactic buy/sell setups.

The other side of this one, the climactic buy, is just the reverse. Multiple black bars in a row, way away from the declining 20-period moving average, and we are going to look for price to snap back to the 20-period moving average.

Let's look at a last few examples. This is my favorite tactic of all. As you go out in the market to look for these Climactic Buy and Sell

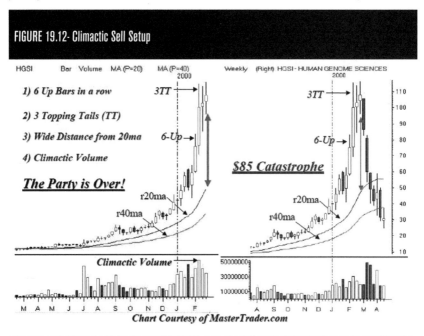

FIGURE 19.12- Climactic Sell Setup

1) 6 Up Bars in a row
2) 3 Topping Tails (TT)
3) Wide Distance from 20ma
4) Climactic Volume

The Party is Over!

$85 Catastrophe

Chart Courtesy of MasterTrader.com

For color charts go to www.traderslibrary.com/TLEcorner

Setups, you will have no trouble spotting them. When it comes to core trading climactic setups, we're talking about major turning points in the stock or in the market. For that reason, I want to include some charts that show the climactic sell setups that occurred during the crash a few years ago.

These are some of the climactic sell setups that formed in the market and in key stocks during that time. The stock in Figure 19.12 is an example of one of those many climactic sell setups. The stock is HGSI from the year 2000. We have six white bars up in a row and this rally has carried us very far away from the rising 20-period moving average. The volume has actually increased on the last of the six bars. Let me talk about that for a moment.

A Discussion of Volume

Volume is a very important part of the Pristine Method. Now that I have said that, let me also say that the uses of volume are often overdone and exploited. The usefulness of volume lies primarily in two occurrences. First, big volume can begin new moves. We call this professional volume.

Second, big volume can end old moves. We call this novice volume. Think about this. The stock has rallied for six straight bars. We know that soon a price is going have to be paid. For every buyer there is a seller. So I want you to think about who is buying the stock on that sixth bar? Do you think that this is a professional market maker or specialist adding the stock to his inventory? Or is it common Joe who just read an article about a tremendous growth rate of the stock and doesn't want to miss out? This is important because when average Joe gets in the stock, it is not going to take much pain to ignite his fear and have him selling for a loss. Multiply that times a few million people and you have the Climactic Sell Setup.

Besides the volume, this chart also shows three topping tails. As you know, this is a sign of big money selling into new highs. With professional money selling and all of the novices already having bought in, there is only one direction for the stock to go—straight down.

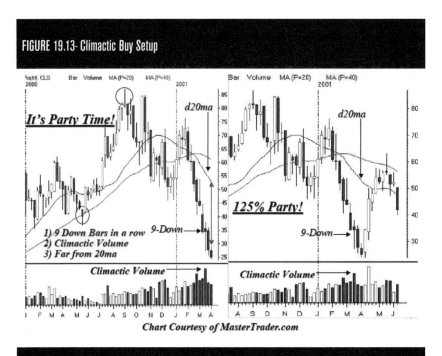

FIGURE 19.13- Climactic Buy Setup

Chart Courtesy of MasterTrader.com

How far is a wide distance from the rising 20-period moving average? It is a visual concept. There is no number I can give you. There are numbers that are given as a guide, but it is detrimental to mention them. You have to learn extended. It means accelerating, not just moving away, and in an almost parabolic form, if that helps. It means it went outside the statistical norm if it is way away from the 20-period moving average. That is where the odds lie. It needs to pay the price.

Does this work the other way around? Of course. Anything technical has a long and a short version. Figure 19.13 is a Climactic Buy Setup. I want you to note some interesting things on this chart. Notice the first circle to the left. Four black bars in a row plus what else? A bottoming tail and in the Pristine buy zone. Much of Wall Street says you can't do that. They say you can't predict with any degree of accuracy what the next move is. Well, after four black bars in a row and a bottoming tail in a Pristine buy zone, trust me, the next move is to the upside. Now let's look at the drop as we get multiple black bars in a row. Nine black bars in a row. That's four bars away from five! That means the snapback is going to be incredibly violent, so the first white bar, I want to be in.

Look at the volume. It is what we call climactic volume, which generally means about twice or more the recent average. It is happening far from the 20-period moving average, so get ready. This forms a huge rally over the upcoming weeks. Of course, where does the rally die? It dies in the Pristine sell zone. You're not an interested buyer anymore. You're an interested seller.

Where can you find these plays? Again, Pristine ESP has changing of the guard plays and bottoming/topping tail plays on the weekly chart. And of course, there are Climactic Setup scans for the weekly chart. Those are among my absolute favorites.

The Four Parts of Every Trade

So now we are in the play. We have shorted the stock, correct? Well, sort of. The truth is there are four parts to every trade. I need to know the entry price, the stop loss price, the target area, and how to manage the trade from the entry and my target. We have just determined the entry price. Let's talk a little bit about each of the other parts of the trade.

> Remember, there are four parts to every trade. You must have them all under your control before you put a penny into any stock.

Stop losses are the second part of the trade to review. A protective stop loss is known as an insurance policy because it guards against the catastrophic loss of hanging on to a losing trade with no action plan in place. A trade should never be entered without knowing where the stop loss is and making sure the trade is exited if the stop loss is hit. For the Pristine Sell Setup, we will always be placing the stop above the entry bar or the prior bar, whichever is higher.

It is a fact that the vast majority of traders who fail to generate profits trading, whether they be long-term or short-term, do so because of the failure to follow stop losses. Now I just gave you the formula for where to place a protective stop loss. It goes above the current entry bar or the prior bar, which ever bar is higher. That is not difficult to understand.

So you need to realize that the traders who do not follow stop losses do not do so because they cannot Figure out where to place a stop loss. There are psychological demons that set into virtually everybody when they trade and these demons often prohibit people from actually stopping the trade, even though they know where the trade should be stopped.

Now, let's take a look at the third element of any trade, the target. If you have noticed, we have determined an entry and stop loss price that will literally be to the penny. Targets are a little trickier, however. We know if we are in an uptrend, we expect to meet or exceed the prior high. Therefore, this will always be our first goal for a target area. The problem is that in strong uptrends, many times the stock may go far beyond that prior high. It is not very satisfying to be out of a trade while it runs several times beyond your intended target.

Incremental Target-Taking

Taking targets is one of my worst demons. For a long time, I was always too quick to take profits, only to see a large chunk of the trade sit on the table as the stock rallied without me. That is why I've become a firm believer in incremental target-taking. What that means, quite simply, is setting multiple targets in the general areas the stock may be likely to run and managing them on the way up.

This allows me to "take home some bacon" today while still leaving some of the trade on for the big move.

Remember our discussion about the micro and macro styles of core trading? Depending upon your style, you will have different objectives in mind for targets. A microtrader will set a target for at least part of the position near the prior high and keep the other part of the trade for as long as stock continues to stay strong. A macro trader may not even have a definite target set, but rather will stay with the trade until it shows signs of strong selling and is far away from the 20-period moving average.

> You may be wondering how to determine a reward-to-risk ratio if you are macro trading. You simply need to approximate your targets based on resistance areas on the chart to determine if a trade meets your reward-to-risk criteria. Naturally, you will then be playing out the trade based on your macro rules, but at least this will give you an approximation of the potential of the trade.

Trade Management Summary

This is pretty straightforward, but there are a couple of options that are available. You need to refer back to our discussion of micro and macro core trading. Depending upon your goals and your style, you will manage the trade differently.

So the goal of trade management is simple. We have an entry point, a stop loss point, and our target area in mind. Our target area may be a trail stop method of some sort. The question of management is if you should step in to protect some of your profits before reaching your final destination. There are different options on how to handle this.

The first option is to not manage the trade any more than your micro or macro style calls for. In other words, let the trade play out and don't interfere with it along the way. This means your initial stop would be your stop for the trade until your micro or macro target-taking rules kick in.

When I first enter the trade, I have my initial stop loss in place. This is where I will exit the stock if it does not move in my favor. At a very minimum, I will keep this stop in place for the first two bars. If I am doing a micro core trade, I will begin raising my stop when I am on the third weekly bar to the second weekly bar, as long as the trade has begun to move away from the 20-period moving average. I will then continue this process every week.

This is known as a bar-by-bar trail stop because every prior bar's high or low becomes your new stop. On a macro core trade, I will leave the trade alone until I see selling pressure and I am far away from the 20-period moving average. If I am not far away from the 20-period moving average, I will raise my stop only when a new weekly buy or sell setup forms.

> When you choose to not manage and let your trade go to a fixed target or stop, it is called an all-or-nothing approach. This should not be dismissed as a management plan.

FIGURE 19.14- Core Trading Summary

Core Trading Combinations

3 to 5 Bar Buy/Sell Set-ups

Can happen with:

1) Topping/Bottoming Tails

or

2) Bull/Bear COG Set-ups

Powerful Core Trading Combinations

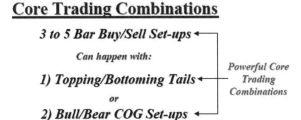

These Combinations can happen:

1) At or Near the 20ma

or

2) In the Buy/Sell Zones

or

3) Far from the 20ma

Location

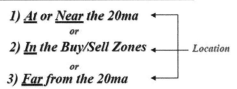

For color charts go to www.traderslibrary.com/TLEcorner

Conclusion

Core trading, like any type of trading, finds success by first finding quality setups. That means a quality trend formed with parallel 20- and 40-period moving averages. Then we want the three- to five-bar drops, the pictures of fear and greed. Then the play is made better if we also have core trading combinations such as topping and bottoming tails or changing of the guards. Figure 19.14 provides a visual summary.

Now these combinations can happen where? At or near the 20-period moving average, or in the Pristine buy/sell zones, or far from the 20-period moving average. Study that summary. This is all you need. You now have the tools to be a successful trader. It's time to trade with confidence. I wish you all the success that you have earned and deserve!

Self-test questions

1. You can do Mighty 20-Period Moving Average Plays with great success if which of the following conditions are met?

   a. The 20-period moving average is rising in a gentle, but steady curve.
   b. The 20-period moving average is above the 40-period moving average.
   c. The stock price has pulled back near the 20-period moving average.
   d. All of the above.

2. Many novice traders are reluctant to sell short, but it's actually easier to make money as a short seller than as a buyer. Why?

   a. The smaller number of traders means you get a bigger share of the pie when the market goes down.
   b. Greed is a stronger emotion than fear in humans.
   c. Stock prices tend to fall faster than they rise.
   d. All of the above.

3. The optimum time to short a stock is when you get a Pristine Sell Setup that features what?

   a. Three or more consecutive black bars, the last one of which has a long upside tail.
   b. Three or more consecutive white bars showing progressively higher lows and higher highs.
   c. Three or more consecutive black bars showing progressively higher highs and lower lows.
   d. Two or more consecutive white bars with extremely long bodies.

4. The Pristine Breakout strategy works best when the stock does what?

   a. Pulls back near the 20-period moving average over three to five trading periods with successively lower highs, then moves up, trading over the prior high.
   b. Trades in a choppy consolidation pattern between the 20- and 40-period moving averages, then moves above the 20-period average.
   c. Moves lower for three or more consecutive periods but with steadily higher highs, then forms a white bar.
   d. Breaks below the 20-period moving average, then rebounds when it nears the 40-period moving average.

5. The Climactic Buy or Sell Setup occurs when a stock does what?

   a. Moves very close to the 20-period moving average on three consecutive trading periods in the same direction.

   b. Moves between the 20-period moving average and the 40-period moving average on four consecutive closes in the same direction.

   c. Moves very far away from the 20-period moving average on five or more consecutive closes in the same direction.

   d. Moves toward the 20-period moving average for three consecutive days, then away from it for consecutive three days.

For answers, go to www.traderslibrary.com/TLEcorner

Glossary

Bearish 20/20 bar: A black bar on a Japanese candlestick chart that is above average in length, with tails that each comprise 20% or less of the length of the total bar (thus, the name "20/20"). The bar's black color indicates that the underlying security closed *below* its opening price. The bearish 20/20 bar is often a signal of an impending or continuing downward price move.

Bearish Gap Surprise Play: A Pristine trading strategy set up by two or more white bars, the second of which is a 20/20 bar accompanied by a climactic surge in volume, followed by an opening downward gap of at least 50 cents. The stock is shorted immediately after the downward gap opening—or, for more conservative traders, only after the stock trades *below* the low reached in the first five minutes following the downward gap opening.

Bear market: A prolonged period during which market prices decline sharply and investors develop a growing level of pessimism; the opposite of bull market. Stocks are generally considered to be in a bear market when prices fall by 20 percent or more, with the move usually triggered by expectations of a faltering economy and, as a result, shrinking corporate profits. Although generally shorter in duration than bull markets, a bear market may last months—or even years.

Bear cycle: A move by the overall market or a specific security in which prices achieve a new high, then pull back to level below the mean or moving average for the period being tracked before rebounding to a level equal to or above the original high. Also known as a high-to-high cycle.

Bear trap: A bullish market situation in which shorts (traders with bearish positions) are caught by a sudden upward price surge. The Pristine Bear Trap play, which can be used over any time period, is set up by a minimum of one 20/20 black bar, followed by an upward gap that takes out the high of the prior period. Bear traps can result in large price moves in a short time period and, as such, require the use of very wide protective stops.

Body: The box on a candlestick chart bar that covers the distance between the opening and closing price for the time period covered. The boxes are colored white when the close was higher than the open, meaning the bulls won the battle that day, or black when the close was lower than the open, meaning the bears came out on top in that day's trading.

Bollinger Bands: A device employed by technical analysts to measure the volatility of a market or security and to determine levels of support and resistance. A moving average of prices is first plotted on a chart, then additional lines, or "bands," are plotted two standard deviations above and two standard deviations below that moving average. This defines a trading channel, which is wider when volatility is high and narrower when volatility falls. When current prices approach the upper band, the market or stock is assumed to be overbought; and when they near the lower band, they are said to oversold.

Breakdown: A bearish move in which prices drop through a strong level of support, thereby triggering additional sharp declines. Breakdowns often signal a trend reversal and mark the beginning of a prolonged downward move or outright bear market.

Breakout: A bullish move in which prices penetrate a level of strong resistance, often a prior high or declining trendline, triggering additional advances. Breakouts often signal a reversal from a bearish trend or the end of a consolidation phase, and mark the beginning of a significant rally or outright bull market.

Bull cycle: A period of activity for the overall market or a specific stock in which prices make a new low, then rally above the mean or moving average for the period being tracked before falling back again to a level near the original low. Also known as a low-to-low phase.

Bullish Gap Surprise Play: A Pristine trading strategy set up by two or more black bars, the second of which is a 20/20 bar accompanied by a climactic surge in volume, followed by an opening upward gap of at least 50 cents. The stock is purchased immediately after the gap opening—or, if you are more conservative, only after the stock trades above the high reached in the first five minutes following the gap open.

Bullish 20/20 bar: A white bar on a Japanese candlestick chart that is above average in length, with tails that each comprise 20% or less of the length of the total bar (thus, the name "20/20"). The bar's white color indicates that the underlying security closed above its opening price. The bullish 20/20 bar is often a signal of an impending or continuing upward price move.

Bull market: A prolonged period during which security prices are rising at an increasing rate amid a climate of growing investor optimism; opposite of a bear market. Bull markets for stocks are generally triggered by increasing economic activity or falling interest rates, both of which tend to promote rising corporate earnings and profits.

Bull trap: A bearish market situation in which longs (traders with bullish positions) are caught by a sudden plunge in prices. The Pristine Bull Trap play, which can be used over any time period, is set up by a minimum of one 20/20 white bar, followed by a downward gap that takes out the low of the prior period. Bull traps can result in large price moves in a short time period and, as such, require the use of very wide protective stops.

Candlestick charts: A style of chart used by technical analysts to plot security price movements over a given trading period, ranging from two minutes to a full trading day, displaying the high, low, opening, and closing price. See Japanese candlestick chart.

Complex sideways correction: A generally flat pattern found on hourly stock charts in which prices trace out an extended series of see-saw movements of roughly equal length and magnitude.

Core trading: A style of market play that typically covers a holding period of several weeks to several months. There are two forms of core trading: The macro style and the micro style. Core trading has replaced the buy-and-hold approach to investing for many investors. Core traders use weekly charts to make entries and exits, quite often focusing on large Blue Chip stocks and major market indexes, especially the indexes or items that mimic the entire market, such as the S&P 500.

Correction: A temporary drop in the price of a stock or the overall market that interrupts an extended rise in prices. Unlike bear markets or crashes, corrections typically entail relatively small percentage price moves—10 percent or less—that occur gradually over a moderate length of time. In strong uptrends, corrections are sometimes considered to be healthy, giving the market time to "catch its breath" before resuming its climb. As such, longer-term investors often view corrections as an opportunity to buy at more favorable prices.

Cup-and-handle pattern: A series of price movements that trace out a chart pattern resembling a cup, with a downward handle extending to the right. The pattern features a short-term top, followed by a gradual retracement that makes a shallow but extended bottom, leading into a modest rally back to the prior short-term high and then another moderate decline. The pattern is usually considered characteristic of base-building periods.

Double bottom: A chart pattern created when a downward trending stock makes a low, rebounds, then falls near the same low and rebounds once again. A double bottom pattern, which resembles a "W," is viewed by many technical analysts as a sign that a stock has tested an important support level and, having made a low, is now poised for a strong upward move. However, a break below the support line created by a double bottom pattern is considered extremely bearish. Opposite of a bearish double top pattern, in which prices movements trace out an "M" on the chart.

Dow Jones Industrial Average (DJIA): The oldest continuing U.S. stock market index and the most widely quoted—though not the most representative—indicator of market performance. The DJIA is composed of 30 large, well-known industrial stocks with leadership positions in various market sectors, all of which trade on either the New York Stock Exchange or Nasdaq Stock Market. Created by *Wall Street Journal* editor and Dow Jones & Co. founder Charles Dow in 1896, the DJIA is a price-weighted average, meaning an $80 stock has more impact on the index than a $25 stock. ETFs and futures based on the Dow are among the favorites of guerrilla traders.

Downtick: A trade for an index or individual security that takes place at a price *lower* than the price at which the previous transaction took place.

Downtrend: A series of declines in the price of a security or the market as a whole. The pattern can be short term, lasting less than a day, or extended, covering days, weeks, or even months. Regardless of the duration, the trend is defined by a series of lower closing prices, as well as a zigzag pattern of successively lower highs and progressively lower lows. An extremely prolonged and severe downtrend—bleeding away 20 percent or more of the market's value—may be classified as a bear market. Opposite of an uptrend.

ECN, or Electronic Communications Network: A computerized order execution system that automatically matches buy and sell orders for specific securities, improving market efficiency and allowing the trading of many securities and index futures after regular market hours.

Elliott methodology: A system of analysis of investment market cycles based on Elliott Wave Theory, which was devised in the 1920s by Ralph Nelson Elliott based on social science trends and the study of mass psychology, which was popular at that time. Elliott's goal was to find an organizing methodology that would explain and predict the otherwise chaotic movement of the stock market. According to his findings, every bullish market cycle—regardless of length—progresses in a price pattern featuring five upward- and three downward-moving waves, although no two patterns are ever exactly alike. In a bear market the dominant trend is downward, so the pattern is reversed—five waves down and three up. Wave Theory has gone in and out of favor numerous times in the years since Elliott's work, but its popularity has risen somewhat with the advent of more effective computer analysis of pricing patterns.

ETF, or Exchange Traded Fund: A basket of securities designed to generally track an index (stock, bond, stock industry sector, or international stock index), the value of which is broken down into units that trade like a single stock. There are more than 120 ETFs, the most popular ones being the QQQ, SPY, and DIA, which respectively are based on the NASDAQ 100, S&P 500, and Dow Industrials.

Extended: A term used to describe a stock that has experienced a series of upward moves or a large upward gap and is thus considered too high-priced to buy based on fundamentals and standard accounting stock valuations. However, guerrilla traders often view such situations as setups for various short-term strategies.

Fibonacci numbers: A sequence of mathematical ratios used in technical analysis to assess the likelihood that a stock will retrace a large portion of an initial price move, find support or resistance at a specific level, and then continue its move in the original direction. The key support and/or resistance levels in any move are determined by drawing a trendline between two extreme points and then dividing the vertical distance by the key Fibonacci ratios of 23.6%, 38.2%, 50%, 61.8%, and 100%. In addition to retracement ratios, other widely used Fibonacci studies—named after Leonardo Fibonacci of Pisa, who first undertook them in the early 13th century—relate to patterns known as arcs, fans, and time zones.

Fibonacci Series: A series of numbers where each number is the sum of the previous two, except for the first two numbers (example: 0, 1, 1, 2, 3, 5, 8, 13, 21, 34). These numbers are widely used in technical analysis to estimate the probable extent of price moves and likely points where reversals may occur.

Flat: A market condition in which a chart shows pattern of price movements that indicate neither a rising nor a declining trend.

Futures contract: A contract creating an obligation between two parties calling for the delivery or receipt of a commodity, currency, or financial instrument (such as a basket of stocks equivalent to the value of a stock index) at a specific date in the future, but at a price that's agreed on today. People commonly think of futures in such agricultural markets corn and pork bellies, but futures have also been developed for financial markets, including the NASDAQ 100, S&P 500, and the Dow.

Gap: A term used to describe the condition when a stock opens at a significantly higher or lower price than it closed at in the prior trading period (most often applied to daily charts). The word gap refers to the empty space that is left on the daily chart from yesterday's close to today's open. A gap is important in guerrilla trading because it often signals the beginning of a major move.

Gap and Crap Play: A Pristine trading tactic set up by two white bars, the latter of which is a 20/20 bar, followed by an upward gap covering at least 50 cents. The play is triggered when the stock subsequently declines to fill the gap, moving 5 to 10 cents below the high of the prior bar. This play works best as a one- to two-day trading tactic using volatile NASDAQ stocks priced above $35 per share.

Gap and Snap Play: A Pristine trading tactic set up by two black bars, the latter of which is a 20/20 bar, followed by a downward gap covering at least 50 cents. The play is triggered when the stock rebounds to fill the gap, moving 5 to 10 cents above the low of the prior bar. This play works best as a one- to two-day trading tactic using volatile NASDAQ stocks priced above $35 per share.

Greed/fear equation: The market is really no more than a battle of emotions, and the colors of the bodies in a candlestick chart indicate which emotion is dominant in any given time period. If the candle is white, greed is in play. If it's black, fear is in play. White means nothing more than the stock closed that bar higher than the open. If it's black, the stock closed that bar lower than the opening price. The opening price and the closing price are the two most important prices of any trading period, whether it covers one minute, one day, one week, or longer.

Guerrilla trading: A dynamic, hit-and-run trading style that relies on well-defined Japanese candlestick chart patterns to find short-term trading opportunities with a high probability of success, regardless of the general direction of the overall market. In fact, guerrilla trading strategies—which typically last from few minutes to one or two days—are often most successful in highly uncertain markets.

Harami cross: A two-period candlestick chart formation in which a candle with a large body is followed by a candle with a smaller body that falls entirely between the top and bottom of the original candle. Generally considered to be a signal that the trend in force is about to change, or reverse, a Harami cross can be either bullish or bearish, depending on the direction of the previous trend.

HOLDRS: An acronym for HOLding Company Depositary ReceiptS, which are service marks of Merrill Lynch & Co., Inc. They are securities that represent an investor's ownership in the common stock or American Depositary Receipts (ADRs) of specified companies in a particular industry, sector, or group. In other words, they trade like a single stock but represent ownership in several stocks in a narrow market sector. Common HOLDRS include the BBH for the Biotech sector and HHH for the Internet sector.

Intraday: Any activity or pattern of price movements that takes place within the course of a single day or market trading session. Intraday action is counter to "interday" periods, which involve analyzing the market or holding a position over more than one daily market session.

Japanese candlestick chart: Originated by Japanese rice merchants, candlestick charts are used both to identify price patterns and construct trend lines, showing a stock's opening price, high, low, and closing price for the specified time period. Like a regular bar chart, the candlestick chart displays the four key price levels for a particular trading period. The primary difference is that the Japanese candlesticks display the information in a way that is much easier to see visually. The area between the opening and closing prices (called the "body") is colored either black or white, depending on whether the stock closed above or below its opening price. This places the emphasis on who won the battle in each time period. Trading that occurred outside the opening/closing range is reflected by single lines—called "tails," "wicks" or "shadows"—that extend above or below the body.

Microtrading: An ultra short-term trading style that involves a holding period covering time spans ranging from seconds to hours. Microtrading does **not** call for holding stocks overnight. This style of active trading goes after small, but frequent bite-size gains. The microtrader typically uses two time frames in selecting potential trades—5-minute charts and 15-minute charts (i.e., the bars on the respective charts represent 5- and 15-minute time periods).

Microtrading phases: Microtraders divide the market day into three segments, known as "phases." Phase 1 extends from the market's opening at 9:30 a.m. EST until 11:15 a.m., when conditions are best suited to tactics based on breakouts (or breakdowns) and reversals. Phase 2 runs from 11:15 a.m. to 2:15 p.m. and is described as the Mid-Day Doldrums, most suited for short-term trending plays or neutral tactics. Phase 3 runs from 2:15 until the market close at 4 p.m. and is again best suited for tactics based on breakouts or reversals.

Morning star: A bullish candlestick charting pattern that shows one large black candle in the midst of an established downtrend, followed by a small-bodied black or white candle and then a large white candle that closes above the first bar's body. Generally considered an early indication that the downtrend currently in force is about to reverse.

Mortgage Play: A bullish or bearish guerrilla trading tactic that can be fairly accurately described as a combination of the Trap Play and the Gap Surprise Play, but that generally involves a longer holding period—often from 3 to 10 days.

Moving average: A widely used technical indicator used to show the average price of a stock or a market index over a given period of time, usually ranging from 10 days (short term) to 200 days (long term). Calculated by deleting the oldest closing price for the period being averaged, adding the most recent closing price and then dividing the total of all prices included by the number of intervals, moving averages are used to both measure momentum and define areas of possible support and resistance. Moving averages, which can also be calculated on an exponential or logarithmic basis, can also help emphasize the trend in force and smooth out price and volume fluctuations (or "noise") that can confuse chart analysis. The 20- and 200-period moving averages are generally considered among the most important timing tools in guerrilla trading tactics.

The Nasdaq Stock Market: Originally a computerized system for quoting securities traded "over the counter," NASDAQ (an acronym for National Association of Securities Dealers Automated Quotation system) has grown to become the world's largest electronic stock market, executing hundreds of millions of transactions daily. Started in 1968 and reorganized in 1971, the NASDAQ had a history of listing emerging companies that might not otherwise have had access to capital markets. However, in 1997, listing requirements were significantly upgraded and NASDAQ split into the Nasdaq National Market (NasdaqNM) for large corporations, including some of America's technology leaders, and the Nasdaq Small-Cap (NasdaqSC) for smaller companies. By 2002, in response to SEC concerns over conflicts of interest, the NASD divested itself of all ownership in Nasdaq, which became a publicly traded, for-profit company in its own right, with stock trading on the NasdaqNM. In 2006, NasdaqNM became an officially recognized global stock exchange operating under the name The Nasdaq Stock Market.

Pristine ESP™: A computerized scanning program into which you can enter the parameters for the guerrilla trading tactics you want to use and then provide you with a daily list of stocks or indexes that meet the criteria for various strategies. Such a package can greatly reduce the time it takes to prepare yourself for daily or intraday trading activity.

Pristine Method: A short-term technical trading system developed by Oliver Velez while Chairman and CEO of Pristine Capital Holdings, Inc., one of the country's premier educational institutions for investors and self-directed retail traders.

Pullback: A decline in the price of a stock or market index from its most recent peak. Such a price movement might be seen as a minor reversal within a prevailing upward trend, signaling a modest weakening in upward momentum. Also sometimes referred to as a retracement when certain mathematical considerations are met.

Relative strength: An indicator used by technical analysts to gauge the momentum of a particular stock by measuring its price change over time and comparing it to the change in a major market index, typically the S&P 500. A stock's relative strength is expressed as a percentage that represents how it performs against other securities. For example, if a stock has a relative strength of 60, it has outperformed 60% of the other stocks over a certain period, usually 12 months. Some analysts consider high relative strength a bullish indicator of future price increases, while others view it as a sign that the stock is "overbought" and ripe for a correction. Also called price persistence.

Resistance: A price level—perhaps marked by a prior high, a trend line, or a moving average—through which a stock has difficulty rising. Buying interest may wane and profit taking by short-term traders kick in as stock prices approach recognized resistance levels. However, penetration of a key resistance level is generally considered a very bullish indicator.

Retracement: A reversal in a stock's price counter to the prevailing longer-term trend. How much of the prior primary move a retracement will cover can be postulated by using Fibonacci analysis to determine the most probable levels of support or resistance.

Reward-to-risk ratio: A calculation used by investors to compare the expected return of an investment to the degree of risk that must be undertaken to earn that return. The ratio is calculated mathematically by dividing the investor's anticipated profit by the amount he or she would lose if the price moved counter to expectations. In short-term guerrilla trading strategies, the reward-to-risk ratio can be defined as the profit to be made on a move from the entry price to the target compared to the loss that would be suffered on a move from the entry to the stop-loss point.

Rotation: In technical analysis, the pattern formed by the price bars in a bar chart as a stock or index moves through various phases of a price cycle—e.g., uptrend, correction, downtrend, consolidation, etc. In broader financial terms, rotation is the movement by investors of money from one or more market sectors or industry groups into other sectors in anticipation of changing economic or market conditions. Also called sector rotation.

RSI (Relative Strength Index): A popular price-following oscillator that, unlike relative strength, compares the internal strength of a single security rather than the relative performance of two different issues. A popular method of interpreting the RSI is to look for divergences, such as when the price of the stock is making a new high, but the RSI fails to surpass its previous top. A divergence between price and RSI is generally considered an indication of an impending reversal. The Relative Strength Index ranges from 0 to 100, but usually tops out above 70 and bottoms out below 30. As with actual prices, penetration of support and resistance levels by the RSI can warn of an impending change in trend.

Short sale: A strategy in which the trader sells a stock or other security that he or she does not own in hopes of buying it back later at a lower price and thereby profiting from the intervening decline in value. A broker or floor trader typically "lends" the security to be sold short, and it is replaced once the security is repurchased (i.e., when the short position is "covered").

Slippage: The difference between the market level or stock price at which you attempt to enter or exit a position and where your order actually gets filled. There is minimal slippage with ETFs or futures representing major market indexes because volume is nearly always high, creating consistent liquidity. However, if you play low-volume stocks that tend to be very erratic, slippage costs can be enormous.

Stochastic: A technical momentum indicator that compares a security's closing price to its price range over a given time period. The model, which is an oscillating indicator, is based on the belief that, as a stock price increases or decreases, its closing prices tend to accumulate ever more closely to the highs or lows for a given period. The indicator's sensitivity to market movements can be reduced by adjusting the time period or taking a moving average of the result.

Stock index: A list of key stocks, usually market leaders, which are thought to be representative of the entire market or of specific segments or industry groups within the market. Some more popular indexes are the S&P 500, the NASDAQ 100, and the Dow Jones Industrial Average.

Stop: An important element of success with guerrilla trading, a stop is a specific price level at which the trader plans to close an existing long or short position in order to cut off growing losses. When used in conjunction with well-defined targets and sound money management techniques, stops are responsible for guerrilla trading's high success rate. **Note:** A stop can also be defined as a price level that represents a probable breakout (or breakdown) point, signaling that a security is now worth purchasing (or selling short).

S&P 500 (Standard & Poor's 500 Stock Index): An internationally recognized index of 500 leading corporations in a broad cross-section of U.S. industries. Although focusing primarily on large-capitalization companies, the S&P 500 is widely regarded as the best single gauge of the American stock market, and an ideal proxy for total market performance with over 80% coverage of U.S. equities.

Support: A price level—usually marked by a prior series of lows, a trend line or a moving average—below which a stock has difficulty falling. Selling pressure may ease and buying interest develop as stock prices approach recognized support levels. However, penetration of a key support level is generally considered a sign of further bearish movement. Support levels can develop over a very short period, such as an hour, or over much longer periods, sometimes holding for a year or more.

Target: An important element of success with guerrilla trading, targets set profit goals for each trade based on the pattern traced out by the underlying stock, index, or CEF during the prior two time periods. When used in conjunction with precise stop points, targets help define the reward-to-risk parameters of every trade.

Technical analysis: A method of forecasting prices of stocks, bonds, futures, indices, or other financial instruments based on chart patterns, price, and volume movements, and numerous other indicators such as open interest, moving averages, oscillators, and cycle analysis. The theory underlying technical analysis is that any influence on the market is already reflected in current price levels—the so-called Efficient Markets Hypothesis (EMH). Technical analysts believe that prices move in trends, that history repeats itself, and that the market discounts everything.

TICK indicator: A measurement done on the stocks of a given exchange, such as the New York Stock Exchange (NYSE). For example, the NYSE TICK measures the number of stocks on the New York Exchange at any moment in time trading on an "uptick" versus those trading on a "downtick." If you have an NYSE TICK reading of +300, it means the number of stocks at this moment in time trading high outnumbered the stocks trading lower by 300. If you have a reading of negative 600, it means that the stocks on the NYSE trading on a downtick at this moment in time outnumber those that are trading on an uptick by 600. Tick indicators are also maintained for the Nasdaq Stock Market and the American Stock Exchange.

Trend: The general direction in which the overall market or the price of an individual stock is moving. Trends can vary in length from intraday to intermediate to very long term. As a general strategy, it is best to trade with trends since trends in motion tend to stay in motion—and in the same direction. Thus, the market axiom, "The trend is your friend." By the same token, although many of the best guerrilla trading tactics involve reversals, it's wise to be cautious about taking positions that rely on price movements counter to the prevailing direction.

Trend line: A chart formation created by drawing a straight line that connects two or more price points and then extends into the future to act as a line of support or resistance. The price points typically represent a series of rising tops, rising bottoms, declining tops, or declining bottoms. A breakout or breakdown through a trendline is generally considered to be a reversal signal.

TRIN indicator: A strength indicator used to measure activity on the New York Stock Exchange or Nasdaq Stock Market. The TRIN, or trading index (also sometimes called the ARMS Index after its originator, Richard Arms), is determined by dividing the ratio of advancing issues to declining issues by the ratio of advancing volume to declining volume. The TRIN works in inverse fashion; with a reading of 1.0 being neutral, while a reading above 1.0 is bearish and one below 1.0 is bearish. TRIN readings can be used as a gauge to confirm the trend of the market and as a timing tool to enter trades in either direction.

Uptick: A trade for an index or individual security that takes place at a price *higher* than the price at which the previous transaction took place.

Uptrend: A series of price increases by a security or the market as a whole. The pattern can be short term, lasting less than a day, or prolonged, covering days, weeks, or even months. Regardless of the length, the trend is defined by a series of higher closing prices, as well as a zigzag pattern of progressively higher highs and higher lows. An extremely prolonged and dynamic uptrend—adding 20% or more to the market or security value—can be classified as a bull market. Opposite of a downtrend.

Void: An area on a chart created when a gap occurs. If the gap is away from the prior price trend, it leaves a visible blank space on the chart, but if the stock gaps into the prior price trend, there is no blank space but it is still considered a void. For strategic purposes, guerrilla traders must be aware that no trades could have been executed at prices in the void area.

Whipsaws: When a stock or index makes a sharp move in one direction—either up or down—then abruptly reverses. Investors frequently lose money, or get "whipsawed," when they buy a rapidly rising stock just before a downward reversal or sell a falling stock just prior to a sudden upturn. Whipsaw movements tend to punish active traders by throwing off misleading buy or sell signals, as well as longer-term investors who "chase the market."

Trading Resource Guide

RECOMMENDED READING

MAKE MONEY TRADING: HOW TO BUILD A WINNING TRADING BUSINESS
by Jean Folger and Lee Leibfarth

Want to be your own boss? Live independently? Take a more active role in managing your money?

That's what a trading business can mean for you -- money, independence, and complete control over your finances. But without the proper education, about 90% of people will fail. That's why this book is essential to your trading success.

As active traders with over 15 years of teaching and coaching experience, Jean Folger and Lee Leibfarth present an organized, top-to-bottom look at what it means to start, run, and ultimately succeed at the business of trading.

Packed with of examples, downloadable code, and worksheets, Make Money Trading gives you unlimited access to all the tools and skills you need to become a profitable, self-sufficient trader.

Item #BCOVx5312378 - $29.95

MONEY-MAKING CANDLESTICK PATTERNS: BACKTESTED FOR PROVEN RESULTS
by Steve Palmquist

This breakthrough guidebook reveals the most effective candlestick patterns and gives you in-depth information on back testing for optimal success. Data that took technician Steve Palmquist years to compile and interpret is now at your fingertips.

Built from PROVEN FACTS, not theory, you'll learn:

• Clear definitions of each selected pattern to remove guesswork and improve performance
• Exactly what you need to know about back testing to increase your wins and minimize your losses
• The impact of various market conditions on the most powerful patterns to remove surprises and increase profits
• Keys to eliminating common testing mistakes that can prevent you from making money
• The candlestick pattern that has shown triple ROI in back testing

Item #BCOVx5510567 - $79.95

MCMILLAN ON OPTIONS, SECOND EDITION
by Larry McMillan

Larry McMillan's name is virtually synonymous with options. This "Traders' Hall of Fame" recipient first shared his personal options strategies and techniques in the original McMillan on Options. The revised, Second Edition, features updates in almost every chapter as well as enhanced coverage of many new and increasingly popular products. It also offers McMillan's personal philosophy on options, and reveals many of his previously unpublished personal insights. Readers will soon discover why Yale Hirsch of the Stock Trader's Almanac says, "McMillan is an options guru par excellence."

Item #BCOVx3362693 - $79.95

STRATEGIES FOR PROFITING WITH EVERY TRADE
by Oliver Velez

An accessible, reliable course for any trader looking for profits in the competitive, dynamic world of trading.

Each section of the book offers: clear examples; concise and useful definitions of important terms; over 90 charts used to illustrate the challenges and opportunities of the market; and how you can take advantage of patterns. Written in the parlance of the day trader's world, you'll enjoy the experience of being taught trading skills by the best of the best.

This focused and effective trading resource features seven key lessons to further a trader's education including: market basics, trade management skills, trading and planning psychology, technical analysis, cutting-edge chart-reading tactics, income- verses wealth-building trades, and classic must-know patterns.

Item #BCOVx5031652 - $49.95

OPTION VOLATILITY TRADING STRATEGIES
by Sheldon Natenberg

No one is more synonymous with volatility trading strategies than Sheldon Natenberg. Through his classic work, Option Volatility and Pricing, this legend in trading success is in great demand for his ability to harness market forces through his calculated approach to trading.

Written in an amazingly accessible style, Option Volatility Trading Strategies untangles the complexity of pricing models and trading strategies and puts them in your hands. This guide levels the field for options traders by showing you:

- An understandable explanation of the Black-Scholes pricing model
- Why theoretical pricing is the most important tool for any option trader
- How to understand probability and why it is a key element in valuing options
- One of the most simplistic explanations of valuation from the most respected source
- How to calculate weekly and monthly volatility and why you need it to make money in options
- Easy-to-understand definitions of the four types of volatility: future, historical, forecast, and implied.

Item #BCOVx5127729 - $39.95

▲ ▲ ▲ ▲ ▲ ▲

To get the current lowest price on any item listed
Go to www.traderslibrary.com

Free 2 Week Trial Offer for U.S. Residents From Investor's Business Daily:

INVESTOR'S BUSINESS DAILY will provide you with the facts, figures, and objective news analysis you need to succeed.

Investor's Business Daily is formatted for a quick and concise read to help you make informed and profitable decisions.

To take advantage of this free 2 week trial offer,
e-mail us at customerservice@fpbooks.com
or visit our website at www.fpbooks.com where
you find other free offers as well.

You can also reach us by calling 1-800-272-2855
or fax us at 410-964-0027.

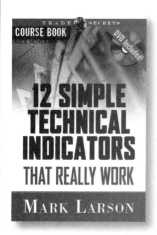
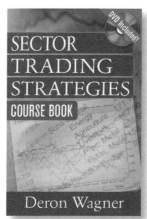

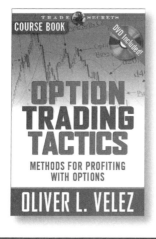
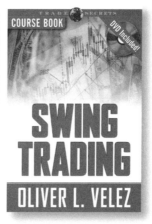

Marketplace Books is the preeminent publisher of trading, investing, and finance educational material. We produce professional books, DVDs, courses, and electronic books (ebooks) that showcase the exceptional talent working in the investment world today. Started in 1993, Marketplace Books grew out of the realization that mainstream publishers were not meeting the demand of the trading and investment community. Capitalizing on the access we had through our distribution partner Traders' Library, Marketplace Books was launched, and today publishes the top authors in the industry; where household names like Jack Schwager, Oliver Velez, Larry McMillan, Sheldon Natenberg, Jim Bittman, Martin Pring, and Jeff Cooper are just the beginning. We are actively acquiring some of the brightest new minds in the industry including technician Jeff Greenblatt and programmers Jean Folger and Lee Leibfarth.

From the beginning student to the professional trader, our goal is to continually provide the highest quality resources for those who want an active role in the world of finance. Our products focus on strategic information and cutting edge research to give our readers the best education possible. We are at the forefront of digital publishing and are actively pursuing innovative ways to deliver content. At our annual Traders' Forum event, our readers get the chance to learn and mingle with our top authors in a way unprecedented in the industry. Our titles have been translated in most every major world language and can be shipped all over the globe thanks to our preferred online bookstore, TradersLibrary.com.

Visit us today at

www.marketplacebooks.com and www.traderslibrary.com

This book, and other great products, are available at significantly discounted prices. They make great gifts for your customers, clients, and staff. For more information on these long-lasting, cost-effective premiums, please call (800) 272-2855, or email us at sales@traderslibrary.com.